# Implementing

# TPM

D1153501

# Implementing

# TPM

## The North American Experience

Charles J. Robinson

Andrew P. Ginder

*Productivity* Press

Productivity Press
444 Park Avenue South, Suite 604
New York, NY 10016
Telephone: 212-686-5900
Fax: 212-686-5411
Email: info@productivitypress.com

Design by William Stanton
Composition and graphics by Rohani Design, Edmonds, Washington
Printed and bound by Edwards Brothers in the United States of America


Library of Congress Cataloging-in-Publication Data
Robinson, Charles J. (Charles John), 1953–
    Implementing TPM : the North American experience / Charles J. Robinson and Andrew P. Ginder.
        p.  cm.
    Includes index.
    ISBN 1-56327-087-0
    1. Total productive maintenance—North America.  I.  Ginder, Andrew P.
II.  Title.
TS192.R63   1995
658.2′02—dc20                                                            95-1327
                                                                              CIP


05  04  03                   9  8  7  6

# Contents

**Publisher's Message  ix**

**Preface  xiii**

**1  Introduction  1**

What Is Total Productive Maintenance?  1
Is TPM Right for Your Plant?  5
What Else Is in This Book?  7

**2  Success of TPM in Japan—JIPM  11**

Japan Institute of Plant Maintenance Background  12
North American Maintenance Improvement Organizations  12
JIPM Awards  14
1991 TPM World Congress  16
North American TPM  20

**3  Preparatory Stage of TPM  21**

Step One: Launch an Educational Campaign to Introduce TPM to
    the Organization  23

Step Two: Create an Organizational Structure to Promote TPM  25

Step Three: Announce Upper Management's Decision to Introduce
     TPM  32

Step Four: Establish Basic TPM Policies and Goals  36

Step Five: Form a Master Plan for Implementing TPM  38

Step Six: Kick Off TPM  41

4  **Implementation Stage of TPM  45**

Step Seven: Improve the Effectiveness of Each Critical Piece of
     Equipment  47

The Importance of Small Groups  53

Step Eight: Set Up and Implement Autonomous Maintenance  57

Step Nine: Establish a Planned Maintenance System in the
     Maintenance Department  62

Step Ten: Provide Training to Improve Operator and Maintenance
     Skills  75

Step Eleven: Develop an Early Equipment Management Program  83

Step Twelve: Perfect TPM Implementation and Raise TPM Levels  88

5  **The Seven Levels of Autonomous Maintenance  93**

Initial Cleaning  94

Preventive Cleaning Measures  99

Development of Cleaning and Lubrication Standards  104

General Inspection  107

Autonomous Inspection  109

Process Discipline  112

Independent Autonomous Maintenance  116

6  **Unions and TPM  119**

What Can TPM Do for the Unions?  122

What Can the Unions Do for TPM?  123

How to Get Union Involvement in the Process  124

7  **Measuring Overall Equipment Effectiveness  125**

Availability  126

Performance Efficiency  128

Quality Rate  134

OEE Calculation for a Single Machine  135

Using the Overall Plant OEE Measurable  136

Calculating a Line or Process OEE Number  137

Accounting for Quality Losses  138
Plant OEE Calculation  144
Corporate or Division OEE Measures  148
Showing the Results of OEE  148
The Power of OEE  149

8 **TPM and Theory of Constraints / Continuous Flow Manufacturing  151**

What Is Continuous Flow Manufacturing?  152
What Is the Theory of Constraints?  154
Theory of Constraints/Continuous Flow Manufacturing and the
    Process Industry  156
How to Correlate Theory of Constraints with TPM  159

9 **TPM and Benchmarking  161**

Finding a Benchmarking Partner  163
Choosing the Benchmarking Team  164
The Benefit of In-Depth Observation  165
Cross-Industry Networking Groups  166
Quantitative and Qualitative Benchmarking  169

10 **Successful TPM Companies  173**

E.I. DuPont  174
Magnavox  175
Texas Instruments  176
Kodak  178
Future of TPM in North America  179

**Appendix: Typical TPM Master Plan  181**

Process Milestones  181
Year-by-Year TPM Goals and Objectives  182
Year One Goals  184
Year Two Goals  185
Year Three Goals  186
Year Four Goals  187
Year Five Goals  189

**About the Authors  191**

**Index  193**

# Publisher's Message

Total productive maintenance as taught by the Japan Institute of Plant Maintenance (JIPM) has achieved worldwide recognition as best in class. Today, TPM is a requirement for all manufacturers who wish to compete in the global marketplace. For the last decade Productivity Press has been committed to translating JIPM's books and training programs for western manufacturers. Our TPM library continues to be our top-selling series. Our customers clearly have no doubt that TPM is essential to their success.

As North American corporations implement TPM, they adjust and modify the method to suit their company culture. As a result implementation models have emerged which make the Japanese methods more accessible and easier to implement for westerners. *Implementing TPM: The North American Experience*, by Charles Robinson and Andrew Ginder, walks readers through their modified JIPM model, which has been honed from their two decades of leadership in TPM implementation in the United States and Canada.

Of special interest to readers will be the emphasis on educating the workforce as the first step of implementation, rather than the third step as in the JIPM model. This ensures that workers and managers alike will understand the implications and value of the program before being asked to commit to implementation. The modification also includes operator teams in the creation of the implementation structure.

The twelve-step program is carefully described and common issues that arise during implementation are addressed. Seven levels of autonomous maintenance are discussed in detail, and a powerful chapter on overall equipment effectiveness provides readers with a clear description of how to calculate and use OEE. A review of the practices at DuPont, Magnavox, Texas Instruments, and Kodak, who have all successfully achieved TPM, offers a glimpse of how world class companies are doing it.

Additionally, the authors include a chapter on the role of labor unions in a TPM implementation program. There is a chapter on how to integrate benchmarking practices to support TPM, which positions TPM solidly alongside western methods of achieving best in class. The authors also offer an interesting discussion of continuous flow manufacturing and the role of the Theory of Constraints in coordinating a TPM implementation in process industries.

It is with great pride that Productivity offers our readers this latest addition to our TPM library. Mr. Robinson and Mr. Ginder bring a depth of knowledge and shopfloor experience to offer a real-world perspective on what works and what doesn't as they cut through the perceived complexity of TPM's comprehensive, companywide approach. We are delighted to be their publisher and grateful for their responsiveness in the development process of this book.

We also wish to thank all those who worked diligently and under great pressure to create this fine product in record time: Karen Jones, managing editor; Connie Dyer, content consultant; Vivina

Ree and Mary Junewick, copyeditors; Susan Swanson, production coordinator; Aurelia Navarro, proofreader; Catchword, Inc., indexing; Bill Stanton, cover and text design; and Rohani Design, typesetting and graphics.

# *Preface*

In today's global economy the survival of companies depends on their ability to rapidly innovate and improve. As a result, an unceasing search is on for methods and processes that drive improvements in quality, costs, and productivity. In today's fast-changing marketplace, slow, steady improvements in manufacturing operations will not guarantee profitability or survival. Companies must improve at a faster rate than their competition if they are to become or remain leaders in their industry.

North American products, practices, and methods were long considered the best in the world. This perception is changing as a result of new competition and economic pressures. Arrogance or self-assurance have devastated specific sectors of our manufacturing base. For example, the Japanese now *own* the consumer electronics industry. Changes in the automotive industry are well documented, and for the first time American-dominated industries, such as computers and aviation, are facing serious challenges by foreign competitors.

Other countries and cultures have proven they can compete successfully in the world marketplace with North American manufacturers. To confront this challenge, enlightened company leaders are benchmarking their organizations' performance and improvement processes against domestic and international competitors. They are adopting and adapting "best-in-class" manufacturing practices and improvement processes. As part of these benchmarking efforts, total productive maintenance (TPM) has been identified as a "best-in-class" manufacturing improvement process.

What is total productive maintenance, and how can it help companies become more competitive in today's worldwide economy? This book answers those questions from a North American perspective. Most other books on TPM have described TPM implementation in Japanese industries. Here we acknowledge the cultural differences between Japan and North America, and how they can affect TPM's successful implementation. It examines how TPM can fit into an overall manufacturing strategy for a North American company.

This book provides plant and division manufacturing managers, business planners, and first-line supervisors an understanding of the complexity and comprehensiveness of the TPM process. While serving as a reference tool for strategic planning, it also meets educational needs of middle and upper management. It supplements works by Japanese authors with guidance and detail on how the TPM process relates to North American plants or facilities.

Since its introduction into North America in the late 1980s, total productive maintenance has been studied, piloted, and, in some cases, partially implemented. Levels of success have varied due to a number of factors. The primary limiter in North American implementation of TPM is the failure of the process to account for differences in how TPM is viewed. In North America, TPM is considered primarily a tactical approach for improving equipment reliability. In Japan, TPM is seen as a universal operating strategy much as North American companies now view total quality management (TQM).

Moreover, cultural differences between Japanese and North American workforces can alter implementation strategies. The basic difference between Japanese and North American workers is the focus of their loyalties. Japanese workers focus on the success of the group, for which they feel a tremendous sense of loyalty. A basic understanding or contract exists between management and workers. Employees agree to limit self-interest and put forth extraordinary efforts for the good of the company. In return, top Japanese companies often guarantee lifetime employment to full-time employees and watch over the well-being of the employees and their families. This social contract promotes teamwork and cooperation, and allows the company and workers to focus on long-term improvements such as TPM.

TPM is a complex, long-term process which must be "sold" to the workforce as a legitimate improvement methodology. A sales pitch is created more easily for a single, homogeneous market segment than for a large, diversified audience. Since Japanese workers usually have a similar ethnic and cultural background, their managers have an advantage in selling the concept. The North American workforce is much more diverse, complicating the selling of new ideas, concepts, or improvement methodologies.

American workers are more self-oriented than the Japanese. Their loyalty is internally focused, and not as automatically or readily transferred to the company. Typically, no contract or understanding exists between them and their employer other than what is negotiated through bargaining units. Most North American companies focus on short-term profitability or quarterly results. Long-term employment is not guaranteed; and, until recently, the concepts of employee empowerment, teamwork, and cooperation were unpracticed in the North American business environment.

Teamwork and cooperation are not unknown to the North American worker. Youths are introduced to these skills from the time they are old enough to hold a baseball bat, football, basketball, or hockey stick. Coaches continually reiterate the value of teamwork in improving competitiveness. Yet North American management has failed, until recently, to tap those competitive skills in the workplace.

For TPM to succeed in North America, both management and the workforce must address issues strategically, while operating in an environment of trust and cooperation. The improvement process must be recognized as benefiting both the company and the worker. The ultimate responsibility for success or failure of the TPM process rests more with management than the plant floor employee. North American workers and their unions can, and will, accept the TPM concepts of teamwork, cooperation, and empowerment, if management provides leadership, security of employment, and reasonable compensation. A major roadblock to successful TPM implementation in North America is the reluctance of managers to change their roles in the organization. For employees to assume power, managers must delegate authority. They must become coaches, facilitators, and teachers rather than autocrats, and information for decision making must be dispersed to work teams rather than being held in the hands of selected individuals.

TPM can help North American manufacturers confront the challenge of foreign competition. This exciting methodology enables companies to gain or maintain a competitive advantage. By taking the concepts of TPM and improving upon them, North America's status as the world's leading economic power can be reaffirmed. It begins, however, with strategic planning and culminates with successful implementation on the factory floor.

# Implementing

# TPM

# 1

# Introduction

## What Is Total Productive Maintenance?

The term "total productive maintenance" was first used in the late 1960s by Nippondenso, a supplier of electrical parts to Toyota. At that time it was a slogan for their plant improvement theme, "productive maintenance with total employee participation." In 1971, Nippondenso received the Distinguished Plant Award (the PM Prize) from the Japan Institute of Plant Maintenance (JIPM). Nippondenso was the first plant to receive the award as a result of implementing TPM, and this marked the beginning of JIPM's association with the improvement methodology. Eventually Seiichi Nakajima, a vice chairman of JIPM, became known as the father of TPM, since he provided implementation support to hundreds of plants, mostly in Japan.

Nakajima describes TPM as "productive maintenance carried out by all employees through small group activities." He considers it an equal partner to total quality management in the attainment

1

of world class manufacturing. According to TPM principles, the responsibility for optimizing equipment lies not just with the maintenance department, but with all plant personnel. For the purposes of this book, TPM is defined as follows:

> TPM is a plant improvement methodology which enables continuous and rapid improvement of the manufacturing process through use of employee involvement, employee empowerment, and closed-loop measurement of results.[1]

Let's consider this definition in more detail.

### TPM Is a Plant Improvement Methodology

TPM is a method for bringing about change. It is a set of structured activities that can lead to improved management of plant assets when properly performed by individuals and teams. Nakajima's twelve-step process for TPM implementation is structured in a "cookbook" format. If followed successfully, those steps will drive performance gains and change plant culture and environment. The culture of a plant does not evolve solely from TPM, but may also be a reflection of other improvement processes that are underway such as total quality management, formal benchmarking, or continuous flow manufacturing (CFM). TPM is not necessarily the optimal improvement strategy for everyone. Later in this chapter, guidelines will be given for determining whether TPM is an appropriate fit for individual plants.

### TPM Enables Continuous and Rapid Improvement

A critical aspect of TPM is that improvements should be rapid as well as continuous. Today's marketplace requires new paradigms. The fable of the race between the hare and tortoise has to be modified. Current and future winners in industry will

---

1. Seiichi Nakajima, *TPM Development Program: Implementing Total Productive Maintenance.* Portland, Oregon: Productivity Press, 1989, p. 5.

combine the quickness and speed of the rabbit with the perseverance of the tortoise. To attain or maintain a leadership position in industry, a company must continuously improve at a rate that is faster than that of its competition. Performance targets must be dynamic, not static. If a company sets goals to reach current performance levels of their best-in-class competitor in two years, they will still lag behind, since their competition will have improved over that same time period. To be best in class, a company must leapfrog its competition by setting goals beyond where their competition is *projected* to be.

### Employee Involvement

Employee involvement is a necessary part of the TPM process. The goal is to tap into the expertise and creative capabilities of the entire plant or facility through the use of small group activities. The total involvement of plant personnel generates pride and job satisfaction as well as financial gains for the organization. Despite the advent of self-managing teams this last decade, true employee involvement is still new and untried at many North American companies. Fear exists over how people's jobs will be impacted from this new management style, and doubts and uncertainties strongly infect both middle management and plant floor personnel. To ensure successful employee involvement, a systematic approach must be designed in which all steps are clearly defined and communicated to involved parties.

### Employee Empowerment

TPM requires employees to take a more active role in decision making and to accept responsibility for the plant and its physical condition. They have a heightened role in defining their job content, along with work systems and procedures. The intent is that each employee takes pride in plant equipment and is proud to be associated with the facility. For example, JIPM recommends that management adopt the theme of "My Plant" to increase the level of autonomous maintenance.

Employee empowerment does not mean that *all* decisions are made by individual workers or small groups of employees. That leads to chaos. Historically, upper management has played the key role in the decision-making process. TPM increases workers' roles in providing input and in making tactical decisions. The most difficult aspect of empowering employees is determining which decisions should be made by management, by workers, or by a combination of the two. Most companies err in not giving workers enough authority, and the proper balance can best be found through trial and error.

### Closed-Loop Measurement of Results

North American plants typically emphasize performance measures that are related to production and financial results. Numbers are tracked, reported by accountants, and made available to select members of the organization. There are two problems associated with classical results measurement. First, the results are not reported to all involved parties. Second, results that are reported do not effectively measure performance. In TPM, the plant establishes "key performance indicators" that measure performance relative to plant goals and objectives. These key performance indicators measure results in areas over which the plant has control. Typically they include availability, quality, productivity, and cost efficiency, as well as measures of the effectiveness of the improvement process itself. The indicators are reported in a closed-loop manner back to the individuals who have the power to impact them. Thus information is placed in the hands of plant floor employees, not just management or staff personnel. Specific reporting methods are discussed in subsequent chapters.

### What TPM Is Not

What is equally important in our definition of TPM is what it does not contain. Notice that the definition does not mention "maintenance." A greatly misunderstood aspect of TPM is that people believe it is only about maintenance because it has the "M" word in its title. TPM does affect the maintenance function greatly, but it also affects *all* other plant functions. TPM is a *production-driven* improvement methodology that is designed to optimize equipment reliability and ensure efficient management of plant assets. Japanese plants are initiating TPM activities in secretarial pools, administrative offices, and even product design departments, areas that are seldom visited by maintenance personnel. The TPM concept of reliability is expanding beyond equipment to serve the total needs of plants by addressing overall organizational reliability.

Perhaps something was lost in translating TPM from Japanese to English. In Japan "maintenance" implies "asset management," not just "repairs." TPM's true meaning or essence might more accurately be captured under the title of "total productive reliability" or "total productive management."

## Is TPM Right for Your Plant?

TPM has gained considerable notoriety since its introduction to the North American market in the late 1980s. A national TPM society as well as an annual conference have been established. Numerous consulting organizations are offering implementation assistance, and hundreds of companies have started some type of TPM activity in their plants and facilities. Although some organizations have achieved remarkable success, progress at many others has stalled. Insufficient planning and lack of management commitment or understanding of the process have hampered many efforts. In other cases TPM concepts simply did not fit in with overall goals and objectives of the company. TPM is not for everyone, and some organizations are too quick to jump on the bandwagon.

Below are criteria to consider when selecting TPM as your improvement methodology.

### Industry Type

TPM methodologies were developed in the automotive industry in Japan, mostly in the Toyota group companies. The concept lent itself nicely to discrete manufacturers with moderate capital assets and a large workforce. Such companies historically had poor records in maintaining their assets. Highly automated, continuous process plants are generally more capital intensive than discrete manufacturers. Due to their huge investments in equipment, they normally manage or maintain their facilities on a more sophisticated level. Despite this higher level of sophistication, TPM is still effective in the continuous process industry. Specific TPM activities and measures must be modified, though, to fit the prevalent concept in process industries of line or unit management as opposed to equipment management.[2] Although some methods are readily transferable, TPM has less applicability to the facility environment (universities, hospitals, etc.) than to production settings. Similarly, some modification of the TPM process and measurables are also required for the power-generation and utilities industries.

## Company or Plant Culture

TPM is most fertile in a stable environment with forward-thinking management. Surprisingly, success or failure does not depend on whether the plant is union or nonunion, but on the level of trust and cooperation that exists between plant employees and management. Management commitment and workforce receptivity are critical to achieving success. Although TPM can be introduced to an organization by workers or first-line supervisors, support from the highest levels of management is required to drive major gains throughout the organization. Some companies resist TPM due to their automatic dislike of anything Japanese. Having taken their share of bumps and bruises from these tough competitors, they want nothing to do with this "Japanese improvement process." Unfortunately, such companies are likely to continue their losing ways. TPM does not belong to any one country. In fact, many of the concepts of TPM have roots in North America. World class companies are innovative, but they also do not hesitate to copy practices and procedures from other leaders in industry.

2. See Tokutaro Suzuki, *TPM in Process Industries*. Portland, Oregon: Productivity Press, 1994.

Numerous companies have successfully built support for TPM-like efforts by simply changing vocabulary and personalizing procedures to fit their unique needs. The basic goals and activities remain the same. Improvement efforts organized around "world class maintenance," "reliability centered maintenance," and "continuous flow manufacturing" are similar to TPM and can be the driving force behind a formal improvement process.

### Present Performance

TPM assumes that basic plant systems are already in place. If preventive maintenance, equipment work order systems, and equipment histories are not already functioning, they should be implemented prior to starting classical TPM activities.

### Strategic Focus

TPM is a long-term strategic initiative, rather than a short-term tactical fix. It will fail if a "program of the month" mentality exists. If an organization has multiple strategies being implemented (e.g., TQM, JIT, ISO 9000, kaizen, continuous flow manufacturing, Theory of Constraints), resources will be stretched. Since most plants have difficulty addressing two major improvement strategies simultaneously, all other improvement activities should be positioned as subordinate and complementary phases of the major strategic plan. TPM has rightly earned consideration as a primary improvement methodology. Its activities fit well with many of the other current improvement philosophies. For example, TPM complements total quality management efforts, because both methods are fueled by employee involvement and empowerment. A Volvo plant in Belgium was one of the first non-Japanese plants to win the JIPM Award. It did so by merging TPM and TQM into one single improvement process.

## What Else Is in This Book?

Chapter 2 notes the extent of TPM implementation in Japan, and describes the relationship of TPM with the Japan Institute of Plant Maintenance (JIPM). Awards and conferences that support and stimulate the improvement process in Japan are also discussed.

Chapters 3 and 4 discuss the TPM process in detail. Although Nakajima divides the classic twelve-step implementation process into four phases,[3] this book simplifies the process into two stages, *preparation* and *implementation*. The "Kickoff of TPM" (normally step six) is treated as part of the preparatory stage, and phase four "stabilization" becomes part of implementation. Also discussed in these chapters is the potential for resequencing the traditional twelve steps to better fit North American culture. Resequencing establishes support for the TPM process prior to announcing commitment to the process.

Chapter 5 explores the seven levels of autonomous maintenance and how they can be used to promote employee empowerment and improve equipment effectiveness.

Chapter 6 addresses formidable challenges to the change process; how to generate receptivity and commitment among plant personnel. Surprisingly, the TPM process is often easier to sell to union representative than to first-and second-line supervisors.

Chapter 7 provides a detailed analysis of the primary TPM measure, overall equipment effectiveness (OEE) or overall machine efficiency (OME). Guidelines are created for calculating the measure for a machine, line, or plant. The chapter also highlights situations in which OEE is not an appropriate measure and discusses alternatives.

Chapter 8 offers examples of North American companies and plants attempting to implement the TPM process. Both successes and failures are examined to determine what elements impacted the varying levels of success.

Chapters 9 and 10 discuss how TPM complements two other widely accepted improvement methodologies—continuous flow manufacturing and benchmarking.

3. Seiichi Nakajima, *Introduction to TPM: Total Productive Maintenance*. Portland, Oregon: Productivity Press, 1988.

In the appendix, an overview draft of the beginnings of a TPM deployment plan is included to assist readers in developing their own individual plan.

The overall purpose of this book is to help companies evaluate TPM as a strategy for achieving excellence in their field. Tactical suggestions drawn from the experience of other organizations will help companies sidestep nonproductive activities. At a minimum, they will serve as thought-provoking exercises and fire up the creative process, so that companies can build their personalized cookbook for TPM implementation.

# 2
# Success of TPM
# in Japan—JIPM

Prominent Japanese businessmen created a furor in recent years with their claim that Americans have become lazy, arrogant, and complacent. Those charges were overblown. America is still the most productive nation in the world, but its position as an economic leader is threatened. Whether the charges are true or not, they reflect a perception that many Japanese managers harbor regarding their counterparts. The reason they feel this way is simple. Americans, suffering from a "not invented here" syndrome, have failed to embrace superior methods and procedures.

In the late nineteenth and early twentieth century, Europe was the economic superpower. Americans not only gladly imported European methods, people, ideas, and philosophies, they modified and improved them to add greater value and produce better products. "Stealing with pride" was a major aid in helping the youthful nation compete with the manufacturing prowess of highly developed countries.

For the past thirty years, the Japanese have copied and refined successful techniques of American corporations. The exchange of information and expertise has been heavily one-sided, as Americans were oblivious to the major gains in quality and productivity by the Japanese. So why don't we turn the tables on them? Why not learn all that we can about their innovative manufacturing methods? The time has come again to "steal with pride." TPM has been successful in Japan. That success needs to be analyzed and refined to provide even greater accomplishments in America.

As stated in chapter 1, TPM had its beginnings at Nippondenso, an electronic and electrical parts supplier to Toyota. The Japan Institute of Plant Maintenance (JIPM), with Seiichi Nakajima as the driving force, quickly absorbed TPM principles and began spreading them to other Japanese plants.

## Japan Institute of Plant Maintenance Background

JIPM is a member of a nonprofit research, consulting, and educational group in Japan called the Japan Management Association Group (JMA). JMA consists of nine professional organizations that focus on managerial needs of individual managers and their companies (see Figure 1). The nine bodies operate independently with the same objective—to enhance the art and science of management in both the public and private sectors.

The JIPM charter states that the entity is "dedicated to developing and sharing methods for increasing organization efficiency and profitability through improved maintenance of manufacturing equipment, processes, and facilities." The initial emphasis of JIPM was preventive maintenance. Although this focus drove significant improvements, new methods were required to take plants to the next level of performance. Since 1971, JIPM has shifted emphasis to the concept of total involvement of all company personnel in equipment and asset management through the concepts of TPM.

## North American Maintenance Improvement Organizations

Several North American organizations and conferences are dedicated to the maintenance professional or maintenance

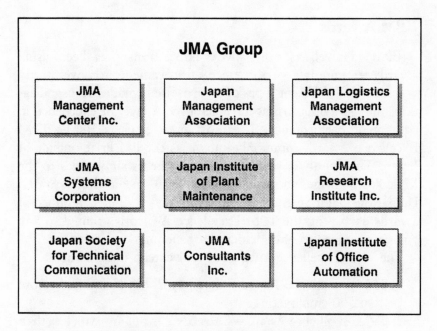

Figure 1. Japan Management Association Structure

improvement. Among the organizations are the American Institute of Plant Engineers (AIPE), the American Institute for Total Productive Maintenance (AITPM), the Institute of Industrial Engineers (IIE), the Society of Maintenance and Reliability Professionals (SMRP), and the International Maintenance Institute (IMI). Each of these groups is designed primarily to assist individuals rather than to support and organize plants or companies. None of them has a nationally recognized award system or benchmark of excellence. A "National Maintenance Excellence Award" is sponsored by *Plant Engineering* magazine and A.T. Kearney, Inc.; HSB Reliability Technologies benchmarks companies under the auspices of the Society of Maintenance and Reliability Professionals; and *Maintenance Technology* magazine recognizes maintenance excellence annually in various plant categories. Unfortunately none of these carries the weight or prestige of the recognition provided by JIPM in Japan.

## JIPM Awards

JIPM (as well as other JMA associations) has been using awards to stimulate performance improvements for over thirty years. Several different types of awards are provided to organizations and individuals that have achieved a level of excellence in equipment performance. The most prestigious is JIPM's TPM Excellence Award, commonly known as the PM Prize outside of Japan. This highly coveted plant honor bears similarities to the Malcolm Baldrige National Quality Award in the United States. Unlike the Baldrige Award, which bestows a limited number of awards each year, the TPM Excellence Award is granted to any company judged to have achieved a benchmark of excellence.

The TPM Excellence Award has four categories of awards.

1. TPM Excellence Award—Category 1 for plants with more than 500 employees.
2. TPM Excellence Award—Category 2 for plants with less than 500 employees.
3. TPM Excellence Special Award for plants awarded the 1st category recognition more than three years ago that show remarkable improvement in TPM activity through unique and distinctive activities.
4. TPM Excellence Award for Consistent Commitment for plants awarded the 1st or 2nd category award more than two years ago that are maintaining, continuing, and improving TPM activities.

The last two awards can be repeatedly awarded to plants that continue TPM activities.

Plants are judged and scored on the ten criteria or core values in Table 1.

The TPM Excellence Awards are given on an annual basis. A preliminary assessment is made by JIPM consultants. Companies submit applications before the end of March. They then develop and submit a detailed activities report by the middle of May. The reports are screened by a committee. Those deemed worthy are

## Table 1. TPM Excellence Award Criteria

| Core Value | Concept |
|---|---|
| Organization and operation of TPM | • Relationship between overall company policy and TPM<br>• TPM policy and target development<br>• Promotional organization for TPM |
| Individual improvements | • Clarification of loss structure<br>• Relationship between improvements and results<br>• Progress and quality of improvement activity |
| Autonomous maintenance | • Preparation of basic condition of equipment and inspection method<br>• Step-by-step development<br>• Effect of autonomous maintenance activity |
| Planned maintenance | • Allocation of work between planned maintenance and autonomous maintenance<br>• Maintenance program and cost effectiveness<br>• Use of equipment audit technique |
| Quality maintenance | • Deployment of quality maintenance<br>• Setting conditions to eliminate defects—control of root causes |
| Early management of new products and equipment | • Maintenance prevention design<br>• Management of new products and equipment |
| Education and training | • Effective skill assessment and educational system for managers, staff, and operators |
| Administrative department | • Reduction of inventory and work in process<br>• Speed of information transmission<br>• Cost reduction |
| Safety, hygiene, and environmental protection | • Safety, hygiene, environmental protection policy, organization, and results<br>• Accident analysis and prevention of recurrence |
| Effect and assessment of TPM | • Comparison of targets and results of TPM<br>• Assessment of TPM's effect from general management viewpoints and future plans |

screened on-site by a team of JIPM consultants and academic and industry experts. A screening committee makes the final judgment in September and the results are announced. In October, the awards are presented in Tokyo.

JIPM provides consulting assistance, and most prize winners purchase varying levels of support prior to winning the award. Some American and European companies such as Ford, Harris Corporation in Florida, and Volvo in Belgium, have used these services.

JIPM also awards other prizes for excellence in service, engineering, equipment, and significant papers.

Approximately four hundred plants received the TPM Excellence Award from 1971 through 1994, with most earning it in the last several years. Nearly half of the award winners are plants that are owned or closely associated with the Toyota group. They were the first large group of companies to totally embrace the TPM process. In 1991, the first two plants outside Japan received the award. The two recipients were a Volvo assembly plant in Belgium and Nachi Industries in Singapore. In 1994, five additional non-Japanese plants received the award, including the first North American-based company (although the plant was located overseas): a Ford Motor Company plant in Charleville, France, won the category 1 award. Other 1994 non-Japanese winners include:

Korea Tokyo Silicon—Republic of Korea
MBK Industrie—France
NEC Semiconductors—United Kingdom
Turk Pirelli Lastikleri—Turkey

Since the TPM Excellence Award is based upon accomplishments rather than methods, it is theoretically possible to receive the prize without embracing the TPM process.

## 1991 TPM World Congress

In November, 1991, JIPM celebrated the 20th anniversary of TPM by holding the first TPM World Congress meeting in Tokyo.

Over 700 people attended the meeting representing in excess of 100 companies from 22 countries. Approximately 150 attendees were from outside of Japan, with 29 from the United States. The largest contingent of overseas representatives were the Koreans. They view their position as similar to Japan's twenty years ago, and have placed a strong emphasis on education. Their efforts are succeeding. Many Japanese companies are more concerned about potential economic or market share threats from Korea than from any other single country. U.S. companies represented included Aluminum Company of America (Alcoa), Alumax, E.I. du Pont de Nemours and Company, Harris Corporation, Mobil Solarenergies, Ford Motor Company, the U.S. Postal Service, Eastman Kodak Company, and Xerox Corporation. The congress provided an excellent forum for an international sharing of improvement ideas and processes.

Most American companies represented at the congress are progressive organizations who recognize the potential of TPM to help safeguard their manufacturing competitiveness. Ford Motor Company, for example, has made a corporate commitment to TPM and is learning as much as possible about it from JIPM. Alumax, recognized as one of the best maintenance organizations in North America by *Maintenance Technology* magazine, is investigating TPM as part of its continuous improvement efforts. Kodak already has taken strides to challenge their major competitor, Fuji of Japan, by installing TPM concepts at several locations; and even the U.S. Postal Service, facing pressure from both private competitors and their own senior management, is considering TPM's potential.

Several presentations at the congress concentrated on the technical aspects of plant maintenance, including expert systems, automation (lights-out operations), and predictive maintenance. In most cases the Japanese technology in those areas is little better than that used at the typical North American plant. In fact, their technology appears to lag behind in predictive maintenance. There were few presentations on computerized maintenance management systems. Apparently Japanese companies have not recognized a need for elaborate maintenance management systems.

Many presentations attended by the authors addressed methods of improving quality and maintenance simultaneously through the use of small, self-directed work groups. Small groups are involved in all TPM activities, even helping to design the improvement process. To promote teamwork and cooperation, the groups consist of plant floor and clerical personnel, as well as plant management, staff engineers, and supervision. In the early stages, TPM involves everyone in an initial cleaning of plant machinery and equipment, and managers play an active role as they don coveralls to work side by side with hourly personnel.

A major point discussed at the congress was how to link improvement efforts in quality and maintenance. At Volvo, for example, quality and TPM are integrated in the concepts of "autonomous quality" and "autonomous maintenance." The plant's entire resources and culture drive continuous improvement in both product quality and the use or maintenance of capital assets. Although JIPM appears to support simultaneous implementation of such complementary philosophies, Nakajima indicated that most Japanese plants already had strong quality-improvement processes in place prior to starting TPM activities. The TPM implementation processes outlined in his books reflect that circumstance. According to Nakajima, the difference between TQM and TPM is that TQM primarily addresses product improvement, while TPM emphasizes improvement of the facility and equipment.

The Japanese consider TPM a neverending process, as new activities are continually initiated. As such, no organization is truly considered to have implemented TPM. Results are measured by comparing performance with the starting point and continually raising targets.

Responding to a set of questions from this book's authors, presenters offered the following information on results from their TPM process.

• The average time from starting TPM activities to achieving the TPM Excellence Award was approximately three years.

- Return on investment from expenses associated with TPM activities (training, consulting, overtime, etc.) averaged seven to one.
- Senior plant management may spend 20 percent of their daily time directly on TPM-related activities.
- Initial cleanup of the plant and equipment can require as much as 160 hours per employee and was often performed on an overtime basis.
- When problems identified during the initial cleanup were corrected, financial benefits up to 300 percent of the initial cleanup costs were realized.
- Each phase of TPM had a theme around which people rallied.

Overall equipment effectiveness (OEE) was used by each of the presenters to help measure the success of their TPM process. This indicator gauges effective use of capital assets by integrating three multiples: equipment availability or uptime, efficiency (speed ratio), and quality performance. Details on calculating this indicator are contained in chapter 7 of this book. Although OEE can be correlated with bottom-line financial results, the Japanese do not use profits as an overall measurable. The reason is that profit has too many associated factors that are outside the control of the plant population. For instance, product demand, the overall economic environment, and the quality of sales campaigns are in most cases outside plant control. The plant does, however, have major control over the effective use of their machines and equipment. OEE is a direct measure of that use.

The Japanese measure not only the results of the improvement process, but also track adherence to improvement activities. For example, since the process has an overall strategy of employee involvement and empowerment, one performance indicator might be the number of suggestions implemented by employees. This is tracked religiously by many Japanese companies on a monthly basis. Most Japanese TPM companies expect to receive a minimum of one suggestion per employee per week, with over half of the ideas being implemented.

In viewing presentations from the Japanese hosts and North American visitors, a glaring difference surfaced regarding the contrasting levels of management support offered the TPM implementation process. North American experiments with TPM are often started at the plant level by an individual who learns of the process and tries to take it forward to his or her area(s) of responsibility. The Japanese usually begin the process with strategic planning at the corporate senior management level and carry it down to the plant. As a result, North American implementations normally start out on a pilot basis or in a small area of a plant, while plantwide efforts are the rule in Japan. These tendencies were also reflected in attendance at the congress. Whereas the Japanese contingent included presidents from a large number of Japanese companies, the only company officer in attendance from North America was a retired vice president. Almost all of the other attendees represented the plant maintenance function or support staff.

## North American TPM

Whereas TPM has proven its value in Japan, pockets of successful TPM implementation are just starting to appear in North America. For TPM to prosper here as it has in Japan, Americans must study the process, visit successful practitioners, and participate in events such as the TPM congress in Japan and annual TPM conferences held in the U.S. co-sponsored by AITPM and JIPM. Intimate understanding of the activities associated with TPM is needed to reengineer the process for North American culture, and senior management commitment must be demonstrated by allocating required time and money. More than pilots and small pockets of excellence are required. The concepts of TPM must become drivers of corporate policy.

A second TPM World Congress sponsored by JIPM will be held in Tokyo in late 1995.

# 3

# Preparatory Stage
# of TPM

This chapter outlines the activities and steps necessary to kick off the TPM process. The twelve-step process described here is consistent with the process originally outlined by Seiichi Nakajima in his book *Introduction to TPM* (see Table 2), although the order of the steps is changed slightly to fit western-style organizations. Whereas Nakajima separates the twelve steps into four stages of implementation, we have consolidated them into two: preparation and implementation. In the preparatory stage, major planning activities for TPM's introduction take place, but on-the-floor changes take place during the implementation phase.

The preparatory stage of the TPM process as modified for North America consists of the following six steps:

1. Launch an educational campaign to introduce TPM to the organization
2. Create an organizational structure to promote TPM
3. Announce upper management's decision to introduce TPM

4. Establish basic TPM policies and goals

5. Form a master plan for implementing TPM

6. Kick off TPM

Notice that the primary difference from the JIPM process is in the order of the first three steps.

> North American companies should begin with education prior to formally committing to the TPM process.

The JIPM process formally commits an organization to the improvement process before most employees really understand its objectives and methodologies. An inherent contradiction exists in mandating an improvement philosophy that is heavily based on employee empowerment. A successful TPM implementation requires top management commitment, but employee input should be actively solicited and evaluated prior to embarking on this

### Table 2. The JIPM TPM Process

| Stage | Step |
|---|---|
| Preparatory | 1. Announce top management's decision to introduce TPM |
| | 2. Launch an educational campaign to introduce TPM |
| | 3. Create an organizational structure to promote TPM |
| | 4. Establish basic policies and goals of TPM |
| | 5. Form a master plan for implementing TPM |
| Preliminary Implementation | 6. Kick off TPM |
| TPM Implementation | 7. Improve the effectiveness of each critical piece of equipment |
| | 8. Set up and implement autonomous maintenance |
| | 9. Establish a planned maintenance system in the maintenance department |
| | 10. Provide training to improve operator and maintenance skills |
| | 11. Develop an early equipment management program |
| Stabilization | 12. Perfect TPM implementation and raise TPM levels |

journey. Recognizing the potential value of TPM, management's initial step should be to create a cross-functional, multi-level committee. This team will include managers, supervisors, support staff personnel and workers from various departments including maintenance, production, engineering, and stores. The objective of the committee is to:

- study TPM methods and results
- identify modifications necessitated by their organization's history and culture
- educate the workforce on the philosophy and how it is likely to affect them and the company

Once management has educated employees about TPM, they should be able to secure their buy-in and commitment.

This chapter addresses the first six steps of the process, with an intent to provide detail beyond that available in *Introduction to TPM*. Actual experiences of companies attempting TPM are also highlighted to show how the process can be tailored to North American industrial environments.

## Step One: Launch an Educational Campaign to Introduce TPM to the Organization

A combination of methods should be employed to educate the organization about TPM. Many training or consulting companies offer general seminars. These sessions normally are offered to the general public at the organization's home office or, on a prescheduled basis, at specified locations throughout the country. Some organizations provide private, on-site workshops for individual companies or groups. Pros and cons exist for the public versus private approach. The informal networking that abounds at public gatherings can be invaluable, as different companies share experiences and people realize they are not treading a solitary path. Private sessions, on the other hand, offer the potential to personalize the materials for the attendees and to analyze issues in greater detail. Having educated an initial group of personnel through one of these methods, many companies adopt a "train the trainer" approach to educate the bulk of the workforce.

These first seminars need only be introductory in nature, since the objective at this point is to generate an awareness of TPM and its value. Opportunities should be taken, however, to define how potential benefits to the company might accrue and how people could be directly impacted. Books may be offered to supplement the workshops, but should not be the only source of education. They lack the anecdotal, personal approach that can be provided by a good seminar leader, and are likely to be left unread. TPM videotapes are also available, and can be especially effective if a trained moderator is available to lead a discussion on the contents.

Although only appropriate for small groups, interplant visits are an exciting way to introduce personnel to TPM. Seeing the activities successfully installed on the plant floor can help sway even the most cynical. Not all employees will be able to share directly in the experience due to time and cost considerations, so care should be taken in selecting respected, credible individuals who can accurately report their impressions of the visit. Networking through professional societies such as The Society for Maintenance and Reliability Professionals[4] and the American Institute for Total Productive Maintenance (AITPM)[5] can help identify potential host plants. The plant tours and associated events can benefit both the visiting and hosting companies if properly organized. Lists of questions and items to be seen should be prepared in advance so that the visits proceed smoothly. This type of activity is widely used in Japan, and, with the advent of benchmarking, is becoming more common in North America.

The objective of initial TPM education is to establish a general awareness throughout the plant of the process and to build support for its concepts. To that end, candidates for education

4. For additional information on the Society for Maintenance and Reliability Professionals contact SMRP Headquarters, 500 N. Michigan Ave., Suite 1920, Chicago, IL 60611-3703, (800) 950-7354.

5. For additional information on AITPM contact Maureen Fahey, Executive Director, (800) 966-5423.

should be drawn carefully from all functions and levels of the organization, including workers and union leaders. The individuals selected to participate in more intensive training should be open-minded and respected by their peers. This core group can transmit key principles faithfully to the remainder of the plant constituency, and are ideal candidates to become internal trainers in later steps of the TPM process.

## Step Two: Create an Organizational Structure to Promote TPM

Once the initial educational phase has been completed, a TPM deployment committee can be organized to study and discuss basic implementation strategies and methodologies. Many plants use executive or staff steering committees to communicate information and to collectively make decisions. The role of the TPM deployment committee is similar, except that plant floor personnel are included as members. The intent is to develop an organizational structure that champions the precepts and activities of TPM. The deployment committee serves as the umbrella for an informal support structure consisting of small groups.

The concept of an overseer group to develop strategies and methods for improvement may be new to some plants, especially if the group includes both management and plant floor representation. Management may doubt the wisdom of allowing the hourly workforce access to strategic planning processes, while workers doubt management's sincerity in soliciting their input. Plants with established quality management programs usually have faced this issue already. If not, patience and persistence will be required of both groups before trust and teamwork develops. Without a cooperative spirit, gains will be slow.

One particular plant in the food processing industry wrestled with the problem of worker involvement in their TPM process. Fearing that TPM was a method for eliminating jobs, the union refused to allow its members to attend the deployment committee meetings. The union's official position was that they would neither endorse nor denounce TPM. After much negotiation, they agreed to observe the meetings without active participation. Through observation, they intended to evaluate management's intent and learn enough about TPM to allow them to take an official stance on the process. After a few meetings, union members who attended the meetings convinced their officers to participate actively in TPM, although the union never did issue an official endorsement of the process.

Membership on the TPM deployment committee should be voluntary, with members who want to improve the plant's work methods and culture. In some instances, there are advantages to including a cynic in the group, as he can provide constructive challenges to new ideas being proposed. As these antagonists become more involved in committee activities, gain greater understanding of the process, and witness management's sincerity, they often embrace the process and become its most vocal supporters. Needless to say, the transformation of such an individual sends a message to remaining skeptics about the value of the process. The majority of committee members, however, should have the following characteristics:

- the respect of their fellow workers
- leadership capabilities
- openness to new and unique methods or ideas
- creativity in problem solving
- strong communication skills
- enthusiasm

Potential committee members should be selected on the basis of the above characteristics and individually approached by a high level manager, preferably the plant manager. Committee members must understand that they will do extra work beyond their regular assignments. Should they hesitate or refuse the invitation to participate despite management's encouragement, membership should not be forced. Voluntary, enthusiastic participants will breathe life into the process, but recalcitrants will waylay activities.

The TPM deployment committee typically consists of 15 to 20 individuals as shown in Table 3.

The role of the deployment committee is to take ownership of TPM, and serve as the primary vehicle for ensuring successful com-

## Table 3. TPM Deployment Committee Structure

| Member | Department | Role |
| --- | --- | --- |
| Plant TPM champion | Plant manager | • Chair the TPM deployment committee meetings<br>• Provide executive support for the TPM process<br>• Arrange and approve resources for the TPM process<br>• Provide continuing support<br>• Communicate and celebrate all successes |
| Plant TPM coordinator | Full-time position from plant staff | • Coordinate all TPM process activities<br>• Publish meeting minutes<br>• Document plans and results<br>• Coordinate resources |
| Process facilitator | Outside resource | • Advise and counsel deployment committee<br>• Independently measure results |
| Maintenance representative(s) | Maintenance first- or second-line supervisor and hourly representative(s) | • Provide maintenance department input<br>• Define maintenance department goals<br>• Coordinate training of production personnel in maintenance practices |
| Production representative(s) | Production first- or second-line supervisor and hourly representative(s) | • Provide production department input<br>• Define production department goals<br>• Develop OEE measurable |
| Engineering representative(s) | Engineering management | • Provide engineering department input<br>• Lead the P-M analysis and maintenance prevention efforts<br>• Coordinate efforts with equipment suppliers |
| Accounting representative | Plant controller | • Equate OEE with bottom-line improvements<br>• Calculate / report financial results of the improvement effort |

pletion of the first six steps of the process. Since the first few meetings of the group are critical to the effort, traditional team-building exercises may be in order prior to attacking the formal agenda. Team building enhances meaningful interaction among members in a relationship that is outside their normal routines. Plant managers and workers interact as equals toward a common objective without concern about authority. Each member's ideas must be considered equally valuable and worthy of thoughtful consideration.

### Initial TPM Assessment

The TPM deployment committee's initial responsibility is to assess current conditions and construct an implementation plan. The assessment is a means of benchmarking an organization's performance against a set of performance standards. These quantitative measures commonly track such items as the percent of emergency work, equipment failure rates, maintenance budget as a percent of replacement asset value, and the OEE of critical plant equipment. An excellent means of starting the assessment is to network with individuals from other plants. The American Institute of TPM and the Society for Maintenance and Reliability Professionals offer such forums. In addition, SMRP provides a general benchmarking for all companies joining the society by comparing them against a database drawn from information supplied by charter members.

### Fundamental Maintenance Practices

TPM is most successful in organizations that already have established good fundamental maintenance practices. Most computerized maintenance management systems, if properly used, provide a framework for such activities. They help organize data and eliminate tedious filing and paperwork. Whether computerized or not, efficient and effective maintenance depends on some sort of organized system. A company's potential success in TPM implementation is enhanced if they have established competence in the following areas.

*Work identification system.* A method is required to identify, document, and backlog maintenance repairs. Normal work requests meet this requirement, as they provide a formal means to specify the problem, identify the work location, and assign a priority.

*Work authorization system.* Once work is formally identified, it must be approved. Different approval levels are required for different size repairs. Small jobs may require only the signature of the work requester, whereas larger repairs may require higher level signatures of supervisors and managers. Many companies define specific spending or approval levels for individual positions in the organization. Extremely large jobs or capital work usually have an approval cycle that is separate from that of routine maintenance.

The work authorization system acts as a filter for all work requests. Duplicate requests are identified and eliminated, and other work may be deferred. Approved repairs are turned into work orders, which are then planned, scheduled, and executed.

*Work order system.* The status of work in process is tracked through a work order system. Once the work request is converted to a work order, money is automatically authorized for labor and materials. A backlog compiles outstanding work orders and identifies total resources needed for completion of repairs. At this point individual work orders are scheduled for repair on either a weekly or daily basis. Labor and materials costs associated with the repairs are charged to the work order as they are incurred. When the repair is completed, actual and estimated costs are compared, and the work order is closed.

The work order serves as a means of communication, as well as a data gathering tool. For instance, the maintenance technician uses the work order to:

- identify the equipment or area requiring work
- communicate with the requester
- diagnose the problem
- order materials
- charge time

*Preventive maintenance system.* Most preventive maintenance systems consist of periodic checks, adjustments, lubrication, and replacement of wear parts. The system triggers work orders to be performed on a time-or cycle-based interval and specifies resources required to perform the work. The system also typically tracks schedule compliance and resources expended, and can correlate these results against equipment reliability.

The effectiveness of the preventive maintenance system depends on two fundamentals. The first is organizational discipline. Preventive maintenance checks and replacement of wear parts must be performed on schedule. The system is not at fault if a failure occurs because oil was not changed when scheduled. The second fundamental is the appropriateness and frequency of identified preventive maintenance tasks. The tasks and schedule intervals comprise the preventive maintenance database. A good database for an effective preventive maintenance system is dynamic, with periodic changes made based on historical performance or changing conditions.

*Equipment history system.* An equipment history documents the complete performance and repair history of a machine. That information should be easy to sort by failure mode, equipment type, cost, and other criteria. Trending and analysis of the information help identify repetitive problems and improve allocation of resources. Information recorded on equipment histories feeds back to the preventive maintenance system, the engineering function (both process engineering and maintenance engineering), and the equipment supplier.

*Cost reporting system.* Successful companies categorize the cost of maintenance by equipment item, area, equipment type, or other meaningful criteria. Ideally, a cost reporting system not only tracks the labor and material expended, but provides a look at the "total cost of maintenance." This includes costs resulting from poor maintenance and malfunctioning equipment, such as the cost of downtime, substandard product, and lost opportunities or customers. Although most plants report on budget compliance, good cost reporting systems provide users with sufficient detail to zero in on specific costs for individual areas or equipment. By understanding where money is being spent or lost, managers can critically analyze performance issues.

The systems outlined above provide a framework for maintenance activities and should be in place prior to implementing TPM. If they are absent or poorly understood and used, the deployment committee should address those fundamentals immediately. The acceptance and growth of TPM is enhanced greatly by these basic building blocks, and knowledge and experiences gained during their development are easily transferred to TPM activities.

### TPM Deployment Plan

The deployment committee is responsible for developing a documented, dynamic plan for all TPM activities. The plan should:

- address major activities, assign responsibilities and deadlines
- identify resource requirements
- define methods of measuring progress

Some corporations have developed very detailed, yet generic TPM plans that are meant to be used as guides for all their plant locations. A sample plan with schedule and task list is included in the appendix of this book for informational purposes. Additional details on how to develop the plan are discussed in step five of the TPM process later in this chapter.

### TPM Committee Structure

Subcommittees or action committees are used to support the deployment committee in completing specific tasks. Their charter might include drafting portions of the overall implementation plan, coordinating benchmarking exercises, or launching a plantwide education campaign on TPM. Once their specific task is accomplished, the subcommittees are disbanded.

Although the action committees are temporary in nature, permanent groups are also created and report functionally to the deployment committee. These groups take responsibility for full deployment of the TPM process through small group activities.

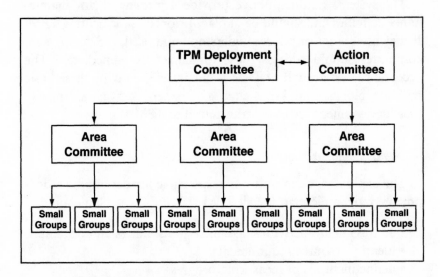

**Figure 2. TPM Committee Organization**

Figure 2 shows the reporting relationship for these interlocking committees. The leader of each small group represents his or her team on the area committee, and area team leaders represent their people on the plantwide TPM deployment committee.

## Step Three: Announce Upper Management s Decision to Introduce TPM

The formal announcement of management's intent to embark on TPM seems a simple task, but it must be positioned and structured correctly for maximum impact on the organization. Employees recognize the significance of the event only if management delivers a clear, consistent message.

## Who Should Make the Formal Announcement?

Highly placed individuals should bear the news to the work-force, and the message should be reinforced by other persons in critical positions. For instance, if the process is to be plantwide, the division vice president and plant manager should deliver a joint message to indicate that the effort has the support of both corporate and plant management. Members of the plant management staff also can demonstrate their support with a few brief words or the mere fact of their physical presence. The unity shown by management will shape the employees' receptivity. That cohesiveness, or lack of it, often determines the outcome of the effort.

If possible, union officers should be encouraged to participate in the announcement, or to endorse the process. Union representatives may be reluctant to take such a visible role at this time, unless they have become sold on the process through involvement on the deployment committee or in other activities. They also will expect some assurance from management that attempts will not be made to reduce head count as a part of the process.

## How Should the Announcement Be Made?

A combination of various methods can be used to announce TPM's formal initiation. A simple method is to either mail or hand deliver a letter to all employees. If hand delivered, managers and supervisors must be coached to provide a consistent, positive verbal message in support of the letter's contents. They should be ready to respond to likely questions or concerns of the workers. Contents of the letter should outline basic TPM objectives, activities, process steps, and expected benefits to the company and its employees. The announcement should emphasize the importance of employee involvement and empowerment, and strongly encourage workers' participation. The letter should be signed not only by the division vice president or plant manager, but also by the plant management team to show their commitment. A sample announcement letter is shown below.

To: All Employees
From: The Plant Manager
Subj: Our Total Productive Maintenance Process

For us to continue to serve our customers to the best of our ability, we must strive for rapid and continuous improvement in all of our work processes and products. As you may be aware, we recently formed a deployment committee representing all levels of our organization to study potential improvement methods. The conclusion of the deployment committee was to adapt total productive maintenance (TPM) to our environment. TPM is an improvement methodology which enables continuous and rapid improvement through use of employee involvement, employee empowerment, and closed-loop measurement of results. The plant management team fully endorses this decision and pledges to each of you to actively support and participate in the TPM process.

In the coming months each of you will receive basic training in the concepts of TPM. Successful implementation of TPM will help us not only meet, but exceed, our ambitious goals in the areas of safety, product quality, customer satisfaction, investment efficiency, and quality of work life. In the next year, we intend to improve the performance of each critical piece of plant equipment through the use of small, cross-functional work groups. Your ideas, creativity, and talents will be critical to the success of these teams. As we proceed further in the process, we intend to increase equipment ownership and performance through the use of autonomous maintenance. Autonomous maintenance is an organized approach for ensuring optimal equipment performance. We will measure our performance and celebrate our accomplishments.

Although it will take several years for full implementation, TPM will become the business philosophy that drives our daily activities. The process will enable our plant to produce more product at higher quality rates. We will strive for nothing less than zero equipment breakdowns, zero defects, zero safety incidents, and zero environmental incidents.

We *must* work together as a team to improve our performance, improve our quality of work life, and become a best-in-class manufacturing plant. We solicit your support in implementing TPM at this plant.

In addition to the written announcement, the decision should be reinforced through a series of meetings involving all employees. The entire management team should attempt to attend each meeting to show support. In unavoidable situations where managers must be absent, a videotape can be prepared in advance allowing them to voice their support. The critical role of the deployment committee and the diversity of its personnel should be emphasized, and the process should be defined in terms of benefits for the employees: greater empowerment and job satisfaction, more job security, and more predictable plant operation. The audience must understand that TPM is a multi-year process that will change the existing plant culture. Skepticism will abound, and management should be prepared to meet tough questions head-on. Management must convince the workers that they are truly committed to the process and will not allow it to become another "program of the month." They can help reinforce the seriousness of their intent by indicating the substantial investments of time and money that will be allocated.

A successful TPM kickoff was held at a two thousand employee plant in the automotive industry. The plant manager held 20 minute meetings during both plant operating shifts with employees in groups of 40 to 50. In the sessions, the manager personally addressed questions and concerns about the improvement process and repeatedly stated her personal commitment.

In addition to, or in place of, such meetings, management may prefer to schedule a special event such as a company picnic. This provides an opportunity to celebrate the start of a new way of doing business.

## Dealing With Negative Sentiment

Despite efforts to prepare the plant population for the TPM announcement, some negative reaction is likely. Typical responses or questions that could arise include the following:

- How can the plant manager authorize overtime to perform initial cleanup activities?
- Is senior plant management committed enough to allocate their time to TPM activities?

- Considering that previous suggestion programs have been failures, is it conceivable that each employee will submit one suggestion per week?

Management must be prepared to answer these and other questions with understanding and sincerity. At the same time they must challenge employees to draw on their creativity in circumventing roadblocks. Potential responses to the questions raised above are as follows:

- Can you help devise a way to perform the initial cleaning activities in less time?
- Don't you agree that managers should spend a large portion of their time on improvements, whether they are related to product quality, the employee work environment, cost control, or TPM? What do we have to do to make that happen?
- Granted, previous suggestion programs have not met our objectives; but a great deal of talent and experience resides in this organization. How can we surface ideas to our advantage?

Rather than dodging questions or concerns, management should respond directly to them. Engaging the employees in finding solutions to their own questions results in committed workers and positive plant floor results.

## Step Four: Establish Basic TPM Policies and Goals

Establishing basic policies and goals of the TPM process is generally more difficult than anticipated. Although it is the charter of the TPM deployment committee to develop the policies and goals, they must have the full approval and endorsement of management.

TPM policies and goals should address the collective needs of employees, customers, and shareholders. Policies are an integral part of the plant's mission, values, and guiding principles. They typically are rules which determine plant or facility priorities as well as how issues are addressed. For instance, a safety policy may dictate that safety related items take precedence over all other repairs. A goal is a specific objective, whose attainment ideally can be measured in a quantifiable method. For example, a plantwide goal might be to achieve an OEE average of 85 percent by a certain date.

Policies and goals must support a company's vision and mission. Whereas a vision should clearly state where a company is heading or wants to be in five to ten years, a mission states why it is in business, what value it adds, and what processes it intends to use to achieve the vision. In other words, a vision is a destination, and a mission is the path. Organizations lacking a well defined vision and mission are rudderless, and a lack of direction is readily apparent to employees. In such circumstances, policies and goals are difficult to develop or cultivate. In actuality, most companies have defined at least a partial vision and mission statement, but they fail to communicate that information effectively to plant employees. Figure 3 depicts the pyramidal structure required to build a successful organization.

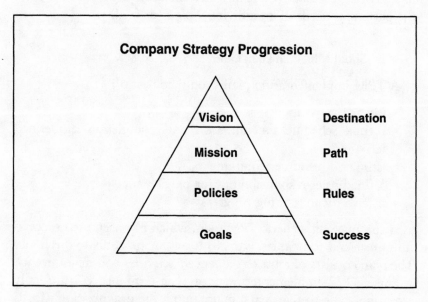

**Figure 3. Relationship Between Vision, Mission, Policies, and Goals**

Establishing TPM policies and goals up front is important in that they serve as the cornerstones for a detailed planning process. Policies are the rules by which people live as they attempt to achieve their goals. Together, policies and goals are the foundation around which management can build employee involvement and empowerment. Employees require freedom to positively impact results, but rules are needed to avoid anarchy and chaos.

## Step Five: Form a Master Plan for Implementing TPM

Developing a master plan for TPM implementation is the most challenging of the preparatory stage steps. A tremendous amount of input and thoughtful analysis are required from each of the TPM deployment committee members. Due to the criticality of this step, many organizations seek outside support and assistance. Drawing on the expertise of someone experienced in TPM plan development saves time and effort and avoids costly missteps. Good TPM facilitators bring a framework plan which then can be modified to meet the particular needs of an individual plant or facility.

### What Should the Plan Look Like?

A TPM implementation plan should consist of:

- a list of activities
- a time schedule for initiation and completion of defined activities
- estimated resource requirements,
- defined roles/responsibilities for participants
- criteria for measuring progress

A summarized, generic TPM plan, which has been used successfully at several companies, is presented as an appendix to this book. The plan consists of a list of sequenced activities and major events.

Since TPM implementation is a long-term process normally requiring three to five years, maintaining the organization's focus can be challenging. The inclusion of multiple short-term milestones in the plan provides additional visibility to the process, as it provides management with the opportunity to formally recognize achievements. Special ceremonies or awards are used by many companies to regenerate enthusiasm and motivate employees in their ongoing efforts.

### Who Should Develop the Plan?

The deployment committee is the primary author of the TPM plan. Usually they will benefit from outside facilitation or guidance, since many of the members are from different departments and are unaccustomed to working together on a team basis. Despite attempts to foresee potential problems in having different groups work together, many issues will not surface until the members sit down to do "nuts and bolts" planning. A skilled, unbiased facilitator accelerates the process by maintaining the group's focus and redirecting unproductive bickering over operational issues or past mistakes. Resentment between members is common. Maintenance personnel often believe the majority of equipment problems are related to operator misuse or abuse, while production counterparts charge maintenance with poor housekeeping and sloppy maintenance repairs or practices. Such rivalries can slow the development of the plan and require that the facilitator allocate a high percentage of time to building the diverse group into a cohesive team with a common objective. Much of the time in initial meetings will be addressed to formal team-building exercises, resulting in little progress on development of the TPM plan.

Although individuals are sometimes frustrated by the apparent slowness of the team building, those activities are critical in setting the stage for a similar change in the entire plant culture. Unless the committee members model teamwork themselves, the workforce is unlikely to follow their lead.

As indicated earlier, actual plan development can be based on generic plans available from consulting groups or companies already embarked on the TPM process. Company-specific details are then verified, developed, and negotiated in deployment committee meetings. The final plan must be dynamic in nature, capable of responding to changes in the marketplace or work environment.

### Who Should Own the Plan?

The deployment committee should promote ownership of the plan by the entire plant or facility. Since the committee represents the majority of plant functions, the plan is easier to "sell" to the rest of the plant population. "Selling" should start during plan development by actively soliciting input from plant personnel. If the committee instead chooses to lock themselves away in an office and operate in a vacuum, any commitment elicited from plant employees will be superficial. Everyone must recognize also that the plan is a living document, subject to change as new conditions arise or additional knowledge is gained.

### What Is the Method for the Plan Development?

The specific methods for developing the TPM plan are decided by the deployment committee. Since the process is time-consuming, committee members must be prepared to spend significant amounts of time in developing and reviewing particulars. The following steps should be helpful in guiding the committee's activities.

1. Start with a generic plan provided by an outside resource, or as included in the appendix of this book. If the plan is drawn from an outside resource, ask one of their representatives to present it in detail to the deployment committee.
2. Focus on the measurable goals developed in step four. The preliminary benchmark established in step two is invaluable in determining whether the goals are achievable, and in identifying potential barriers to their attainment. Additional benchmarking may be required to cover additional goals not covered in step two.
3. Anticipate weekly four-hour meetings of the deployment committee to modify and hone the plan. Additional meetings will be required of small ad hoc groups as they wrestle with individual responsibilities and assignments such as selecting pilot areas or defining training requirements. The facilitator or other outside resource can incorporate revisions to the

plan. The entire process is accelerated if participants prepare for meetings by reviewing minutes, documenting their input for discussion, and by adhering to the meeting agenda.

4. When all parties agree, publish the plan and make it available to the whole plant or facility for feedback.

### How Long Will It Take to Develop the Plan?

Time required to develop the plan may range from four to twenty weeks depending on such variables as team dynamics, management commitment, and current work rules and environment. If the committee can avoid temptations to accept the generic plan carte blanche, implementation pains will be eased. A well-conceived and defined plan requires more time and effort, but is of paramount importance in gaining buy-in from plant personnel. Employees must believe that the plan is modified and workable for their special environment

## Step Six: Kick Off TPM

The TPM kickoff consists of a formal celebration, in which the purpose of the process is announced to the outside world (customers and suppliers) as well as plant employees. It differs from step three (Announce Upper Management's Decision to Introduce TPM) because it is a public announcement held in conjunction with a celebration. Correctly performed, the event generates an increased awareness of the process and a groundswell of enthusiasm. The event symbolizes a new beginning in which historical thought patterns, practices, and paradigms are challenged. Management effectively drives a stake in the ground in announcing a new way of conducting business. In Japan, a TPM kickoff frequently consists of the following activities:

• Outside vendors, suppliers, customers, local government officials, worker families, and senior company management are invited to the plant or facility for a formal ceremony to celebrate the kickoff of TPM.

- Speakers, representing all levels and functions of the plant, detail reasons for proceeding with TPM and define anticipated activities and results.
- Symbols of the process are dedicated to the workers. Items such as jackets, decorative TPM fountains, and recreational areas are unveiled and dedicated to the workers for their efforts in establishing the improvement strategy.
- Refreshments and entertainment are provided to make the ceremony enjoyable for all attendees.

Elaborate celebrations of this type are unusual in the North American business environment, and many people dismiss them as nonsense or an unnecessary extravagance. Some companies, though, have used a similar approach in initiating new quality management processes. In those situations, management recognized the need to create a lasting impression on their people regarding the new way of doing business. The typical approach on kicking off new projects in North America is much more subdued, often consisting only of a series of internal meetings for managers and supervisors. This reflects a "business as usual" approach, whereas the intent should be to celebrate the birth of a management style that will re-create the company and drive it to new performance levels. Except for groundbreaking ceremonies, North Americans are accustomed to celebrating achievements after the fact, when milestones are achieved. Commitment to TPM reflects a commitment to breaking with past practices and unfettering people's full creativity and talents. Such a commitment is worthy of celebration. North American companies should consider a celebratory kickoff for the following reasons.

- A major celebration reinforces the commitment of management personnel to the change process. Having stated their support publicly and unequivocally, management can back away from their promises and commitments only with considerable loss of face. Recognizing that their credibility is on the line, most managers will be extremely reluctant to deviate from the stated objectives; but instead will make herculean efforts to drive the process through to success.

- A celebration ignites enthusiasm and commitment among attending employees. Although this excitement must be nurtured throughout the process, the first major step has taken place. An important aspect of the event is that all attendees hear firsthand a consistent message. Rather than taking a chance that the message be diluted or changed, which frequently occurs when information is dispersed through multiple meetings, management can communicate a distinct plan, clarify misconceptions, and squash rumors before they start. They can drive home the message that TPM will not be another "program of the month."
- The uniqueness of the celebration helps it stand out in the minds of the workforce. The fact that such major events are uncommon for most companies serves as an indicator to employees of the gravity of the situation, and underlies the company's seriousness about upcoming changes in the organization and its practices.

Timing of the event is crucial. Normal excitement will build in anticipation of the event, and activities should be planned to take advantage of people's heightened expectations. Then management can build on the momentum generated by immediately embarking on highly visible TPM activities.

The preparatory stage is only the beginning point of the TPM process. Although much organizational work is accomplished at this time, actual on-the-floor improvement activities have yet to be initiated. If proper planning has taken place in the preparatory stage, though, immediate and positive results will materialize.

Many individuals and companies try to leapfrog the preparatory phase, usually with unfortunate results. They attempt to work immediately on tasks which can potentially result in measurable improvements. For instance, individual supervisors attending TPM seminars frequently begin activities on their own with little overall planning, guidance, or support. The results can be disappointing and compromise the process in the future. Even when successes are achieved, they are difficult to transfer across the organization, since other individuals were not involved in the initial planning.

For example, a product line supervisor in a plant was excited about the possibilities of TPM after attending a workshop. The supervisor purchased TPM books for the employees in his area and initiated several new activities. Unfortunately he started without advance planning; had no firm, established goals; and lacked support from his management. The process stalled quickly because immediate results failed to materialize. Eventually TPM was rejected as an improvement methodology for the entire plant, due to its failure to succeed in one area. The real problem was not any inadequacy of TPM, but in the process of its implementation. The preparatory stage lays the foundation for the success or failure of the TPM process, and it is only with great risk that management can forgo the detailed planning it requires.

# 4

# Implementation
# Stage of TPM

In the implementation stage TPM moves from planning to on-the-floor activities to improve equipment performance. In Japanese plants, this stage typically unfolds over a two and one-half to four year time period. Obviously management commitment is critical to sustaining such long-term activities. North American companies face a special challenge here, in their tendency to frequently rotate or promote managers. This flux in organizational structures and management personnel endangers long-term improvement processes such as TPM, even when replacement personnel are committed to maintaining the same philosophy.

Several North American companies have built sustained commitment to their improvement processes. The Q1 quality process at Ford has been widely documented and copied, as is the Quality Systems Review process at Motorola. These companies made true corporate commitments to quality. Since the entire company was committed, success or permanence of the process did not depend on any individual or small groups. Q1 became the beacon for

Ford's quality focus. The company developed the concept, advertised it to the world through television commercials, and instituted a system of rewards to ensure that their plants and suppliers implemented the process. Similarly, the Quality Systems Review process is the primary driver for Motorola. Although not as widely advertised as Ford's Q1, Motorola's activities are as intense and are considered crucial to the company's long-term profitability and survival.

Since TPM was only introduced into the United States in 1988, few U.S. plants have completed the implementation stage. In fact, that part of the process might be considered never-ending. Once TPM activities are initiated on the plant floor, their repetition and expansion never cease.

The final six steps of the TPM process consist of the following:

7. Improve the effectiveness of each critical piece of equipment
8. Set up and implement autonomous maintenance
9. Establish a planned maintenance system in the maintenance department
10. Provide training to improve operator and maintenance skills
11. Develop an early equipment management program
12. Perfect TPM implementation and raise TPM levels

JIPM separates these steps into two stages. Steps seven through eleven are considered the implementation stage, and step twelve is identified as the stage of stabilization. This book treats all six steps as part of the implementation stage.

As indicated earlier, the detailed, on-the-floor activities of this stage typically unfold over two and one-half to four years. Milestones need to be established throughout this time period to sustain people's interest and motivation. By establishing clear targets and tracking performance against them, TPM focus is enhanced. Efforts should be made to document and recognize completion of specific steps in the process, as well as noting improvements achieved in actual equipment performance. The plant should visibly celebrate the attainment of milestones, and show how they fit within the master plan.

## Step Seven: Improve the Effectiveness of Each Critical Piece of Equipment

Step seven involves a concerted effort by all plant personnel to improve the reliability and performance of critical equipment in the production process. The intent is to maximize the value of capital assets. A TPM indicator, overall equipment effectiveness (OEE), has been developed to help evaluate equipment performance. The measure comprises three variables: availability or uptime, quality performance, and capacity utilization or running speed. To provide full return on investment, equipment must meet design specifications for each of those variables. The higher the OEE, the more efficiently the machine is operating. Chapter 8 details suggested methods of calculating OEE.

The importance of tracking equipment performance using a measurable such as OEE can not be overstated. Sports provide apt analogies of the importance of keeping score. Every athletic event has an accepted method to define winners and losers. Imagine a scenario in which scores were not tallied. Would the players exert themselves? In tennis, for instance, you can see readily the different levels of effort expended in tournament matches as opposed to practice sessions. The players push themselves harder in matches, especially on critical points. The focus of athletic endeavors is to be the best. No matter what skill level, participants play to win, and the score is the indicator of their success. Years ago fewer statistics were kept for all sports. Whereas batting averages, earned run averages, and fielding percentages were common then, they have now been supplemented by a wide range of new measures that can overwhelm many observers. Managers have found, though, that proper analysis and use of the new indicators provides them with a competitive edge. You have to keep score to maximize your chances of winning. We are a product of what we measure.

The OEE is the best method for keeping score in a plant or facility. A method should be established for compiling each machine's OEE, as well as an overall OEE for the line, process unit, or entire plant. The scores should be posted for all of the workers to see,

and reward systems should be established to recognize achievements in improving the OEE.

Correlate the OEE measurable with other plant indicators such
as financial measures (see Table 4). Although such comparisons
can be difficult, they prove extremely valuable. An improvement
of one percentage point in OEE can be expressed in additional
profits or reduced costs, thereby serving to justify capital expenditures. The company controller or financial staff should be charged
with the task of investigating and establishing the links of OEE to
profits for each process unit or line.

The value of linking the OEE to financial information can be
highlighted by an example drawn from the food industry that is
summarized in Table 4. A food processing plant needed to measure
the financial opportunities for improvement in their process. They
determined that the plant functioned with an average OEE of 50
percent. Significant losses from quality problems and equipment
failures contributed to this low OEE level. The plant was in a sold
out condition, but as a result of poor equipment performance, they

## Table 4. Example of OEE Correlation to Financial Results

**OEE Correlation to Financial Results**

- Current plant OEE = 50%
- Current plant sales revenue = $150 million
- Possible plant sales revenues at 85% OEE = $150 million × 85% ÷ 50%
    = $255 million
- Profit margin on incremental sales volume = 30%
- Increase in profit = 30% of ($255 million − $150 million) = $31.5 million
- 35% increase in OEE = $31.5 million
- Or each OEE percent increase is worth roughly $1 million.

were contracting with outside services to package additional product. Initially the company considered building or purchasing additional capacity, but the OEE indicated that the potential additional capacity already existed in their current plant. The value of this untapped potential was enormous. The total annual sales revenues of the plant were in the range of $150 million. Improving the OEE to 85 percent, a goal proven attainable by many Japanese discrete manufacturers, would result in a sales revenue increase of $105 million. The profit margin for the plant on an incremental case out the door was approximately 30 percent of each sales revenue dollar. Therefore the incremental profit for increasing the plant OEE from 50 percent to 85 percent was 30 percent of $105 million, or $31.5 million. In rough terms, each percentage point increase in the plant OEE improved earnings before taxes (EBT) by slightly less than $1 million. Those numbers grabbed the attention of corporate management and became a key criteria in determining capital investments.

Although a 50 percent OEE may appear extremely low for a production facility, it is typical of many discrete manufacturing operations analyzed in North America. It also reflects the enormity of the tasks and rewards that await us.

The following steps are guidelines on how to improve equipment effectiveness in a plant or facility. They are based on assigning activities and responsibilities to small work teams that are charged with continuously upgrading the performance of specific equipment.

### 1. Select Equipment

Define which pieces of equipment in the plant are candidates for performance measurement. Critical process equipment or bottlenecks are certainly candidates. Other possibilities include equipment that performs marginally, impacts safety, or becomes a bottleneck when producing at maximum plant capacity.

## 2. Measure Loss

Devise a method of measuring and tracking the OEE on each of the candidate machines. The loss is equal to the missed opportunity resulting from operating at less than 100 percent OEE. Quantifying the loss provides the basis for setting priorities as outlined in step three.

## 3. Prioritize and Plan Improvements

Based on criteria collected in step two, prioritize underperforming machines and develop a plan to improve their performance. Priorities should be established according to two factors. The first factor addresses the difficulty or expenditure of effort to improve the performance of each piece of equipment. The second factor establishes the importance or criticality of the equipment to the process, which can often be expressed in financial terms. Equipment criticality should be ranked on a numerical scale of one to five, with one indicating the highest level of importance. Similarly, each piece of equipment should be ranked on a scale of one to five according to the degree of difficulty in improving its performance. Degree of difficulty is based upon estimates by the small groups assigned to the equipment. A score of one would indicate that the equipment has problems that are the easiest to solve. By multiplying the two factors together, each machine is assigned a number, with the lowest being the number one priority. Refer to Figure 4 for an example of the prioritization process.

## 4. Study and Correct Problems in Small Groups

Use small work groups to identify, isolate, study, and take corrective action on equipment problems. A number of analytical and problem-solving methodologies are available for use in these activities. Among the most popular outside of TPM are fault tree analysis, failure mode and effects analysis (FMEA), fishbone analysis, and reliability centered maintenance. Traditional TPM methods include Pareto loss analysis, factor analysis combined with

## Equipment Candidate List

| Equipment Candidate for Performance Elevation | Criticality | Difficulty of Improvement | Priority Product |
|---|---|---|---|
| Injection Molding Machine | 3 | 4 | 12 |
| Hydraulic Press | 2 | 3 | 6 |
| Tube Mill | 5 | 4 | 20 |
| Transfer Line | 1 | 2 | 2 |
| Grinder | 2 | 3 | 6 |
| Punch | 4 | 3 | 12 |
| Lathe | 1 | 1 | 1 |
| Vertical Punch | 4 | 1 | 4 |
| Deburring Machine | 3 | 5 | 15 |

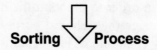

## Sorting Process

## Resulting Priority Sort

| Equipment Candidate for Performance Elevation | Priority Product |
|---|---|
| Lathe | 1 |
| Transfer Line | 2 |
| Vertical Punch | 4 |
| Hydraulic Press | 6 |
| Grinder | 6 |
| Injection Molding Machine | 12 |
| Punch | 12 |
| Deburring Machine | 15 |
| Tube Mill | 20 |

**Figure 4. Prioritizing Equipment Candidates for Performance Elevation**

5-why root cause analysis, and P-M analysis for chronic or persistent losses with complex causal patterns.[6] Each of the methods searches for and corrects the "root causes" that result in equipment failures or "hidden defects." The theory is that a hidden defect may result in a number of different types of symptoms. If only symptoms are treated, the hidden defect or root cause may never surface.

The repair history of an diesel-engine-driven process pump serves as an example. Over a three year period, the engine had been frequently repaired. Two starter motors, three cooling water pumps, and a main seal (due to oil leakage) were all replaced. Finally the root cause of all of the failures, a warped flywheel, was discovered. The warped flywheel was destroying the starter motors, and its vibrations damaged the water pump and the main seal. This problem was not diagnosed until a competent mechanic analyzed all of the symptoms in order to pinpoint the hidden defect

Most companies assign the technical portion of formal problem-solving activities to engineers. TPM traditionally delegates this responsibility to cross-functional project teams made up of production personnel, operators, and maintenance and engineering staff. The collective experience of such groups can lead to a more accurate diagnosis of chronic failures. Note that such detailed analysis will require additional time from maintenance craftspeople, time that becomes available when production operators take on repetitive, routine maintenance tasks of cleaning, adjusting, and lubricating.

### 5. Monitor Progress and Share Results

Like product quality, equipment performance must be monitored continuously and religiously. The process for measuring equipment performance must be institutionalized, so that it is a normal part of the equipment operator's responsibility. When successes are achieved, the events or activities leading to the improvement should be studied, documented, and shared with others. In that manner pockets of success can be transplanted throughout the organiza-

---

6. For more detail on these methods, see *TPM Development Program* (Nakajima), *Training for TPM* (Nachi-Fujikoshi), *P-M Analysis* (Shirose et al.), and *TPM in Process Industries* (Suzuki), all from Productivity Press.

tion. A similar transfer of information should take place regarding activities that fail, so that employees can avoid repeating errors.

### 6. Reevaluate Priorities and Continue Improvements

Continually prioritize the list of underperforming machinery and initiate activities for continuous improvement. The success of organizations depends on their ability to make rapid and continuous improvements. Small work groups must be reminded periodically to reevaluate their priorities, and to take an "evergreen" approach to their business practices. For example, they should continuously assess the effectiveness of their preventive and predictive maintenance procedures. The cost and time involved in completing the tasks should not outweigh the potential financial gains from reduced downtime. Unfortunately, most companies decide to evaluate their preventive maintenance practices in one fell swoop every three or five years. The task proves overwhelming, since a few employees are assigned responsibility for conducting the review and recommending changes in a short time frame. Instead, the groups should borrow a technique from maintenance stores. Historically, most stores performed an annual physical inventory for accounting purposes. A major time commitment was involved, and the inventory count had little lasting impact on improving parts accuracy. Now many stores have switched to cycle counting. Under this approach, a portion of the inventory is always being counted throughout the year. This eliminates the major year-end labor requirement for an annual inventory, and provides more timely feedback to stores personnel regarding the accuracy of their parts management. The cycle counting approach can be applied to an analysis of preventive and predictive maintenance by challenging work groups to evaluate a set percentage of tasks every month or quarter.

## The Importance of Small Groups

The above six activities necessitate the formation and effective use of small groups on problem-solving activities. Although such activities are the foundation for employee involvement and empowerment, most companies have not structured themselves to take advantage of the expertise that resides within their plants. North American manufacturing traditionally has been organized in a top down structure, with the plant manager at the apex of the pyramid. Reporting directly to the plant manager were the departmental or functional managers of production, maintenance, engineering, and administration. This structure, based on functional capabilities and responsibilities, continued through all levels of the maintenance organization, as even supervisors and crews were segregated along craft lines. During the last ten years many changes have occurred gradually. Rather than supervising a single craft, foremen have taken responsibility for multi-craft crews; and instead of eight to fifteen different craft designations, many crafts are now consolidated into technical versus general mechanical groups. The distinction between operators and craftsmen also has blurred. As employees broaden their skill sets, they are performing tasks that historically were beyond their capabilities and job definition.

Plant organizational structures are decentralizing the maintenance function as they transition to a structure based on area management. Although a centralized maintenance group is still retained, a number of maintenance foremen or crews report to production. The benefit of such a structure is that an area manager has greater control over the resources that determine the area's success or failure. Interfunctional teamwork between operators, engineers, and maintenance craftsmen is enhanced, as the groups are part of a team with a common objective.

The evolution from the traditional pyramidal structure to one based upon teamwork, communication, and cooperation is difficult. Management must become less autocratic and more participative if small group activities are to flourish. Since success in TPM implementation depends greatly on the success of small group activities, we need to understand their essence.

### What Is a Small Group?

A small group is any cross-functional work team charged with working together to improve plant performance by solving problems and managing specific plant areas, machines, or processes.

The team usually consists of five to twelve members who are delegated sufficient authority and resources to manage their area of responsibility. The groups are permanent parts of the organization, and normally include production operators, skilled craftspersons, and first-line supervisor(s). Temporary assistance or support is frequently solicited from other groups such as engineering, finance, or outside vendors.

### How Are Small Groups Formed?

Small groups do not form spontaneously, but are created through specific actions of plant management. A primary responsibility of the TPM deployment committee is to organize and promote initial small group meetings and to provide training on small group dynamics, goal setting, task assignment, documentation, and results measurement. This non-technical training is necessary for the effective kickoff of small group activities.

A typical scenario for forming small groups is as follows:

- The deployment committee decides that a small group is needed to address performance problems of a specific machine.
- Operators and craft personnel are either assigned or requested to serve on the team along with a first-line supervisor.
- TPM trainers conduct several two-hour training sessions on team building and group rules, so that personnel understand the basics of meeting management, budgetary guidelines and authority, and setting performance objectives. The workshops also provide an opportunity to reinforce understanding of the TPM process and to address worker concerns on how the activities may affect their job.
- The group meets independently with a facilitator to discuss potential approaches to improving the performance of the troubled machine. Data collection methods and data review techniques are an integral part of the process.
- Ideas are discussed and evaluated according to formal problem-solving techniques, and recommendations are tested on the plant floor. The group meets regularly to evaluate results and reports to management any changes in machine performance.

For small groups to succeed, plant management must remove barriers that result from the traditional pyramidal organization. Since production and maintenance normally report through different structures and management, work rules and practices differ. In addition to basic difference in daily activities and tasks performed by the two functions, work hours, break times, and shift schedules also may be out of sync. Small work groups tend to be more successful when work rules are consolidated and differences between the two categories of worker are minimized.

### How Do Small Groups Function?

Small groups interact both formally and informally. Formally, small groups meet on a periodic basis to discuss issues and make decisions using the following guidelines:

- *Define the issue(s)*. Decide what is to be attacked or improved. Designated improvement targets should be consistent with improvement goals developed in the preparatory stage.
- *Measure present performance*. Develop a quantitative measure of present performance. OEE is a good measure of success in most cases. However, other items such as efficiency and cost measures may be equally valid.
- *Establish goals*. Again, these should be quantitative in nature, such as improving OEE by so many percentage points in the next three months.
- *Brainstorm ideas*. Solicit and gather input from all group members on how to separate symptoms from root causes of problems. Evaluate the merits of various improvement options.
- *Decide on a plan*. The plan may require gathering more data, changing operating parameters, or redesigning equipment.
- *Implement the plan*. Change activities or equipment as defined in the plan. Management should be prepared to fund ideas requiring capital investment, and budgets or spending authorities should be set up for the team.
- *Measure the results*. Continually monitor changes in performance resulting from implementation.

- *Recognize the success.* Document and reward groups for achieving objectives.

Many small group meetings require an experienced facilitator, who may or may not be the first-line supervisor. The facilitator may be drawn from an outside organization, or the position may be rotated among members of the team if they are trained in that skill. Since the intent of the interfunctional teams is to benefit from the members' diverse experiences, the facilitator must encourage everyone's active participation. The relative merits of each suggestion should be reviewed and discussed thoroughly.

The timing, frequency, and duration of meetings initially should be established by the TPM deployment committee, with the small groups taking charge as they become involved in the process. In Japan, production is stopped for planned small group activities, or meetings are held offshift and participants are paid overtime.

## Step Eight: Set Up and Implement Autonomous Maintenance

Autonomous maintenance is the process by which equipment operators accept and share responsibility (with maintenance) for the performance or health of their equipment.

The seven levels of autonomous maintenance include:

1. Initial cleaning
2. Preventive cleaning measures
3. Development of cleaning and lubrication standards
4. General inspection
5. Autonomous inspection
6. Process discipline
7. Independent autonomous maintenance

For detailed steps on how to implement autonomous maintenance, refer to chapter 5. Below is a discussion on the purpose, potential barriers, and changes which result from the implementation of autonomous maintenance.

Maximum performance and productivity is possible only if equipment is maintained in a clean, organized, and disciplined workplace. Although easy to understand, this concept is hard to implement. A large investment in both human resources and training is required initially to follow through on autonomous maintenance. Most Japanese plants begin the process by using workers on overtime hours to perform an initial cleaning of their machines. All levels of employees, including the plant manager, participate in the initial cleaning activities.

Many North American plants and facilities have failed in their attempts at autonomous maintenance. An example of potential difficulties can be seen in the travails of a discrete manufacturing plant in New Jersey where corporate management mandated TPM implementation. The facility, under great pressure, went through an abbreviated preparatory stage. Small group activities were initiated and equipment performance (OEE) was tracked. The plant deployment committee, lacking representation from lower levels of the organization, became extremely uneasy at the notion of autonomous maintenance. The large investment (approximately 20 percent of their annual maintenance budget), potential union resistance, and concerns about their ability to sustain any gains from the initial cleaning process unnerved the committee. They decided to suspend the autonomous maintenance process and focus only on improving equipment effectiveness. The plant was nervous about implementation of autonomous maintenance and its emotional impact on the plant's union employees. Since they had failed to incorporate worker input and participation into the deployment committee, they were now forgoing major benefits of autonomous maintenance that show up as improved equipment reliability and greater product throughput.

Every plant must evaluate the value of autonomous maintenance for their organization. Although it provides major returns on investment for many companies, there are exceptions. This was proved at one discrete manufacturing site. This facility exhibited excellent maintenance basics, good equipment performance, a high degree of employee enthusiasm for continuous improvement, and an enlightened management team. The management team examined autonomous maintenance and judged that the training requirements and cost of downtime while performing the training far exceeded the potential benefits. Projected training requirements of 120 hours per employee were estimated to cost the plant over $4 million. This expense could not be recouped by squeezing extra capacity from equipment. The possibility existed, though, that the plant could have broken the required training into much smaller increments and used on-the-job techniques to limit training costs while still attaining the performance gains.

Many plants have piloted autonomous maintenance on a particular process or equipment item, but have been unable to convince management or the plant population of the value of expanding the process throughout the facility. Several initial barriers are:

- The perception that autonomous maintenance violates work rules established between management and labor through collective bargaining or historical practice. This is a real issue which must be addressed through analysis of contract language and honest discussions with the union leadership before a pilot is initiated.
- Management's unwillingness to invest the effort and resources required to change present work practices. This is a true test of management's commitment to the process. Too often, when times toughen economically, management becomes unwilling to invest in autonomous maintenance.
- The perception by maintenance craftspeople that autonomous maintenance is a method of eventually reducing head-count by reducing their scope of duties and responsibilities. Assurances must be offered to maintenance craftspeople regarding their job security.
- The belief that cleaning equipment is a useless exercise, since it will be dirty again in a short period of time. It should be emphasized that autonomous maintenance entails not only an initial cleaning of the equipment, but also implementing actions to keep the equipment clean.
- The perception that management is not concerned about plant housekeeping except when dignitaries visit.

These barriers can be negated by careful planning and open,
communication with the employees. The first issue to be dealt with
is fear—namely, fear of losing one's job or having greatly diminished responsibilities. If possible, plant management should issue a
policy stating that:

> Implementation of autonomous maintenance will not cause
> anyone in the plant to lose their jobs.

The management team must believe in and stand behind this
policy. Successful TPM implementation will improve the plant's
profitability and should lead to a more stable job environment. If
management anticipates personnel reductions through layoffs as a
result of autonomous maintenance, they do not understand the
concept of TPM. Unless management is able to allay concerns of
potential job losses from autonomous maintenance, chances of
success are greatly diminished.

The second issue that must be dealt with is to answer the question "What's in it for me?" Table 5 provides sample answers to
this question from the perspective of production operators, skilled
craftspeople, engineering personnel, and first-line supervisors.
When customized for each plant or facility, the chart serves as a
tool to "sell" the autonomous maintenance process. Emphasis
should be on the fact that learning new capabilities enhances the
overall value of the employee to the organization. The general
answer to the question of "What's in it for me?" is:

- a more stable job
- additional knowledge and capabilities
- a safer, cleaner, more rewarding quality of work life
- an increased voice in plant operations

Table 5 shows how autonomous maintenance gives people
greater responsibility, which should create a more satisfying work
environment. Improving employees' skills through training
enhances their ability to handle increased levels of responsibility.
Additional education takes place as groups draw on the base
knowledge already residing in the plant or facility. Small group

## Table 5. Autonomous Maintenance Work Activity Changes

| Job Title | Present Work Responsibilities | Additional Responsibilities After Autonomous Maintenance (Small Group Activities) |
|---|---|---|
| Production operator | 1. Operate machine<br>2. Start up machine<br>3. Shut down machine<br>4. Clear jams in machine<br>5. Report machine malfunctions<br>6. Maintain a safe environment<br>7. Check product quality<br>8. Fill out SPC charts<br>9. Log production output | 1. Accept ownership of machine<br>2. Maintain machine cleanliness<br>3. Maintain organized work environment<br>4. Perform machine checks<br>5. Perform machine lubrication<br>6. Log and trend machine performance (OEE)<br>7. Participate in small group activities |
| Skilled craftsperson | 1. Perform machine checks/adjustments<br>2. Replace worn parts<br>3. Lubricate machine<br>4. Respond to machine shutdowns<br>5. Repair/replace broken components<br>6. Rebuild/overhaul machine | 1. Maintain and review equipment histories, including performance (OEE)<br>2. Analyze equipment failures for root cause identification<br>3. Specify equipment modifications to increase performance<br>4. Interface directly with machine suppliers to increase performance<br>5. Specify PM requirements<br>6. Train production operators in PM activities<br>7. Participate in small group activities |
| Plant engineer | 1. Monitor machine performance<br>2. Specify machinery changes<br>3. Interface with machine supplier<br>4. Specify new machinery<br>5. Specify PM tasks<br>6. Specify part requirements | 1. Define plant engineering strategies<br>2. Coordinate operating philosophies<br>3. Benchmark equipment performance<br>4. Participate in small group activities |
| First-line supervisor or work team leader | 1. Manage production operators<br>2. Manage production schedule<br>3. Approve work requests | 1. Lead small group activities<br>2. Consolidate equipment performance measurables<br>3. Communicate performance results to plant management<br>4. Communicate plant management's strategic intent to small groups |

activities are an apt medium for dispersing existing knowledge across a broader base of the plant population. The training is often documented in the form of single-point lessons which are developed and taught through small group activities. These are lessons of short duration focusing on a single point or concept that can be taught quickly on the floor or in a classroom environment.

Although small group activities are used in step seven to improve the effectiveness of each piece of machinery, they are especially critical to implementing autonomous maintenance. They function as a knowledge sharing pool that transfers necessary skills to the production operators. As such, the dynamics and teamwork associated with small groups must be fully operational for autonomous maintenance to take root.

## Step Nine: Establish a Planned Maintenance System in the Maintenance Department

Enlightened North American companies have been striving for the past several decades to move from reactive to proactive maintenance. Planned maintenance is defined as maintenance activities which are performed to a predetermined schedule of activities. Planned maintenance activities evolve in four stages: reactive maintenance, preventive maintenance, predictive maintenance, and maintenance prevention. Whereas reactive maintenance entails waiting until something breaks before initiating maintenance activities, preventive maintenance involves periodic checking, adjusting, and replacing of parts to prevent equipment failure. Predictive maintenance is the measuring of process variables and equipment condition, so that potential problems can be forecast. Maintenance prevention, on the other hand, eliminates the need for maintenance through improved design of equipment. Most North American companies have established preventive maintenance systems, with procedures and schedules developed for at least their critical equipment. Although the scheduled procedures may not address the actual needs of the equipment or may have unreasonable intervals, at least some regular checks are scheduled and completed. In addition, many medium-to large-sized plants have experimented with predictive maintenance in the form of either vibration analysis, thermography, or lube oil analysis. A very select number of companies have also begun developing the concept of maintenance prevention.

With the major focus that has been placed on planned maintenance systems, it is surprising that only a few North American companies have truly optimized their practices through detailed review and data analysis. The goal of optimization is to receive maximum benefit from limited maintenance resources. Technology is available to automate and manipulate data in a maintenance optimization process, thereby facilitating step nine of TPM. As an example, Kvaerner Engineering UK, Limited, based in Slough, England, has developed and marketed a set of software tools called "Optimus," which analyzes maintenance and cost data to help in optimizing the maintenance function. The tool is used effectively by many companies in Europe and is beginning to be used in North America by organizations such as Weyerhaeuser and Texaco. It provides financial models of the maintenance function by categorizing data such as:

- the cost of performing maintenance
- the probability of failure as a function of time
- the cost of fixing an equipment failure
- the cost of downtime

The maintenance cost models actually simulate equipment operation and calculate the lowest total costs. This is accomplished by evaluating the costs of performing repairs against the potential financial gains or losses accrued through changes in equipment performance. Additionally, Dr. Andrew Jardine of the University of Toronto has done work on models to optimize maintenance cost.

To understand the concepts of a planned maintenance system, we should first define some of the terms associated with the concept.

### Reactive Maintenance

In a reactive maintenance (RM) system, the maintenance department responds to equipment malfunctions or breakdowns. The problems are fixed as quickly as possible, so that equipment becomes operational. Often the repair may be temporary in nature. Reactive maintenance is the least efficient operational mode, overall, for the maintenance department, although in some cases it can be cost effective. For instance, it may be more effective in some situations to replace lighting as it fails; while in other cases, all lighting should be replaced on a periodic schedule.

### Preventive Maintenance

Preventive maintenance (PM) activities are designed to prevent equipment failures and ensure reliability. PM tasks are performed at predetermined periods with established methods, tools, equipment, and time estimates. Common examples are equipment checks, adjustments/calibrations, periodic replacement of equipment wear parts, and overhauls or rebuilds. The aim of PM is to maintain equipment in a new or on-spec condition. PM usually requires shutdown of the machine to perform the tasks. It is a form of planned maintenance in that needed tools, materials, skills, and time requirements are established in advance, and the actual shutdown of equipment is coordinated with production. The frequency with which PM is performed varies, but typically is based on set time intervals, actual equipment run time, or production cycles. Many PM tasks, including lubrication, adjustments, and cleaning can be carried out by production operators through the autonomous maintenance process.

### Predictive Maintenance

Predictive maintenance (PdM) is the periodic measurement and trending of process or machine parameters with the aim of predicting failures before they occur. Whereas a preventive maintenance activity such as lubrication may prevent a failure, predictive maintenance activities are focused on predicting or forecasting potential equipment problems. If a potential failure is forecast, corrective action can be taken prior to the equipment malfunction. The most common types of PdM include:

- vibration analysis
- thermography
- eddy current testing
- oil analysis
- liquid penetrant testing
- ultrasonic testing
- acoustic emission testing
- radiographic testing

Other forms of PdM include trending of process data such as temperature or pressure. PdM is used as a triggering device for corrective action, with the tests usually performed while equipment is operational. Since predictive maintenance focuses on actual condition of the equipment, it can be more cost efficient than PM. Worn parts are not replaced unless measured operating conditions indicate that replacement is required. The principles behind PdM were developed by the U.S. Navy's submarine fleet. The navy used to take submarines to dry dock for a complete overhaul or refit at set intervals. Although the cost of the repairs was an issue, the major concern was that approximately half the submarine fleet at any given time was in dry dock for repairs that often proved unnecessary. To surmount this obstacle, navy engineers devised tests to test the integrity of systems. The technology advanced to such a level that submarine dry dock time has been cut by two-thirds.

## Maintenance Prevention

Maintenance prevention (MP) is a relatively new concept that is a key concept of TPM. MP is based on the precept that most maintenance requirements for a piece of equipment are determined in its design. If equipment designers and engineers place more focus on maintainability, operability, flexibility, and robustness, many of the typical maintenance requirements for the equipment can be eliminated. The car battery is a simple example of the process. Ten years ago most car batteries required periodic addition of distilled water into the cells for continued longevity. Now, due to improved design and construction, most car batteries are "maintenance free." As another manufacturing example, most small electric motors are now equipped with sealed bearings which eliminate the need for periodic lubrication.

Improved equipment design has led to the incorporation of self-diagnostic capabilities, so that machines can alert operators to problems. Another type of maintenance prevention is the simplification of maintenance tasks, so that little or no skill is required to perform them. A typical example of both self-diagnosis and simplified maintenance tasks is the clearing of paper jams on a copy machine. A paper jam used to require a service call to the "key operator" or maintenance contractor. Now the machines are designed with imbedded step by step diagnostics and simplified instructions on how to clear the jam. MP is the systematic application of these techniques to low-and high-cost production machines.

A brief comparison of the various types of planned maintenance just described is included in Table 6.

One challenge of the TPM deployment committee is to optimize the different systems of planned maintenance and integrate them with TPM. Although the overall goal is to move away from reactive maintenance and towards maintenance prevention, the optimum level of maintenance varies with each process and each equipment item in the process. Critical pieces of equipment benefit more from the application of PdM and MP. PM and even RM may suffice for less critical items. For example, it would not be practical to establish a PdM system on a door hinge or a pressure gauge. PdM also is more efficient in an around-the-clock process, since the tasks can be performed while the equipment is in operation. In a two-shift operation, PM checks can be performed on the third shift while the equipment is down.

| | Reactive Maintenance | Preventive Maintenance | Predictive Maintenance | Maintenance Prevention |
|---|---|---|---|---|
| System description | 1. Maintenance department responds to equipment malfunctions and breakdowns | 1. Periodic adjustments and checks 2. Periodic replacement of wear parts 3. Periodic overhaul | 1. Periodic measurement and trending of equipment and process parameters | 1. Equipment design is based upon minimal maintenance requirements |
| Characteristics | 1. Inefficient maintenance department 2. Unpredictable equipment operation 3. All maintenance work is unplanned | 1. More predictable operation 2. More efficient maintenance department | 1. Predictable maintenance requirements 2. Planned and scheduled equipment repairs | 1. Close relationship with equipment suppliers |
| Examples | 1. Light bulb replacement | 1. Changing oil and filters | 1. Vibration analysis | 1. Sealed bearings in small electric motors |
| Results | 1. Steady degradation of equipment performance | 1. Maintain level of equipment performance | 1. Maintain equipment performance with minimal disruption to production | 1. Continually improving equipment designs |
| Maintenance department responsibility | 1. Respond to emergencies 2. Get production back on line | 1. Keep machines running by checking, replacing, and overhauling 2. Perform checks during down times | 1. Log equipment parameters 2. Trend data 3. Predict equipment repair cycle | 1. Input to equipment design 2. Minimize and eliminate maintenance requirements |

Table 6. Planned Maintenance System Transition

All types of maintenance systems can be optimized, even reactive maintenance. An example is an engineering study that was designed to optimize the maintenance and operation of a drill press. The operation required that twelve holes be drilled simultaneously into a sheet of metal, and the study was intended to identify the optimal replacement interval for the drill bits. Three types of bit failures were prevalent.

- *Infant mortality:* A certain percentage of the bits never worked at all or failed after drilling only a few holes.
- *Random conditions:* These failures were found to be associated frequently with operator error.
- *Normal wear:* As the bits approached the end of their normal life cycle, the failure rate increased dramatically.

The existing practice was to replace each drill bit as it failed, an example of reactive maintenance. By taking data over a period of weeks, plant personnel were able to calculate the probability of failure over time for a single drill bit. They also were able to calculate the cost of the failure in terms of lost production, idle operator time, and maintenance replacement of the failed drill bit. Potential costs were calculated for each of the following scenarios:

- run to fail; replace failed bit only
- replace all bits daily; replace failed bits as they fail
- replace all bits every two hours; replace failed bits as they fail
- replace all bits every four hours; replace failed bits as they fail
- replace all bits every shift; replace failed bits as they fail
- replace bits individually after eight hours of operation or when they fail
- replace all bits at each failure

As it turned out, the optimal method was to replace all bits in the drill at each failure. At machine restart, all bits were fresh and much more likely to permit the drill press to run for an extended period of time without failure. This single operational change saved the plant in excess of $25,000 per year per machine. Since the plant had more than forty of these drill presses, total savings were $1 million. In this particular situation, both reactive and preventive maintenance practices were optimized at the same time.

Success lies in a company's ability to determine the optimal balance of resources and activities for each of the four systems of maintenance. To find that balance, extensive data collection and analysis is a prerequisite. Without good data the drill bit analysis described above would have been impossible.

## Computerized Maintenance Systems

Computers are helpful in establishing an information base and for organizing that information in an easy to use, retrievable, electronic filing cabinet. Many excellent computerized maintenance management systems on the market do more than an adequate job. In fact most commercially available packages have more features and functions than many organizations can use effectively. Lists of the most popular packages are regularly published in trade magazines such as *Maintenance Technology*, *Plant Engineering*, or *Plant Services*.

In selecting a computerized maintenance management system, the buyer must remember that the system is not the solution. Just like any other maintenance tool, it has the potential for misuse or abuse. The *effective use of any system* is the solution.

Effective use of a computerized maintenance system requires discipline. Accurate lists of equipment and spare parts must be complemented by well-defined maintenance procedures. Constant and consistent updating of databases to reflect current conditions should be a joint responsibility of the small TPM teams and maintenance department. The following are guidelines in implementing, upgrading, or optimizing a system:

1. Build a general set of specifications for the software based on maintenance goals. For example, if the goal is to reduce downtime, the package should provide downtime reporting and tracking. The specific package selected should handle the plant's size requirements: number of maintenance craftspeople, inventory line items, number of equipment items, and

work order transaction volumes. Many companies look for the system with the most advanced features, which invariably lie unused after the installation. A manual system also can be effective, although compiling and analyzing data is much more manageable through computerization.

Refer to Table 7 for a list of parameters and potential features that should be considered in choosing system specifications.

2. Consider carefully any decisions to change or customize a vendor's off-the-shelf system. Customizing a system jeopardizes the plant's ability to take advantage of future upgrades. Many companies have spent hundreds of thousands of dollars customizing a system to fit their special needs, only to revert back to the vendor's base system at a later date to take advantage of additional functionality in later versions. Some customizations or additional interfaces will be necessary, but they should be kept to an absolute minimum.

3. Build an accurate master equipment list immediately. The list will note each equipment item that is to be maintained as a separate entity. Figure 5 details the data structure for a typical master equipment list.[7]

4. Create a recommended spare parts list that supports the equipment included in the master equipment list. The recommended spare parts list may contain all of the items stored in your maintenance stockroom, as well as those that are not stocked but frequently used. Data on frequently used parts can then be used to specify outside purchases. Figure 6 details the data structure for a simple spare parts list.

5. Ensure that good PM plans are created to maintain equipment. The plans should encompass all equipment included on the master equipment list, and should include frequency of scheduling, coordination of tasks to be performed, and level loading of resource requirements throughout the year. The

7. Charles Robinson, "Designing a Master Equipment List," *Plant Engineering Magazine*, Cahners Publishing Company: January 8, 1987.

## Table 7. Potential Maintenance System Specifications

| System Requirements | Functional Requirements |
|---|---|
| • Hardware: type of computer and operating system | • Master equipment list: database and organizational requirements |
| • Database: requirements by brand or type | • Planned maintenance work flow: work order life cycle |
| • Procedural language: preferences in programming language | • Preventive/predictive maintenance: work flow requirements |
| • Response time: maximum allowable computer response time | • Corrective/scheduled maintenance: procedures for handling reactive maintenance |
| • User interface: user interface desired—mouse, touch screen, windows | • Scheduling: an automated scheduling capability |
| • Graphical output: graphics and standards required | • Equipment histories: ease in updating histories and correlating data |
| • Distributed data processing: client and server technology requirements | • Bill of materials: equipment sub-levels and spare part lists |
| • System level documentation: The following documentation should be provided: | • Maintenance stores: spare part inventory control |
|   ➤ User reference manual | • Cost analysis: analysis of total equipment life cycle cost |
|   ➤ Systems administrator guide | • Reliability and maintainability data: calculations of mean time between failure and mean time to repair |
|   ➤ User training manuals | |
|   ➤ Database documentation including data flow model and table structures | |
|   ➤ User training database | |
| • Security: various levels of system security required | |
| • Help: on-line help requirements | |
| • Reports: routine and ad-hoc reports required | |
| • Interfacing: interface requirements with groups such as accounting or inventory control | |

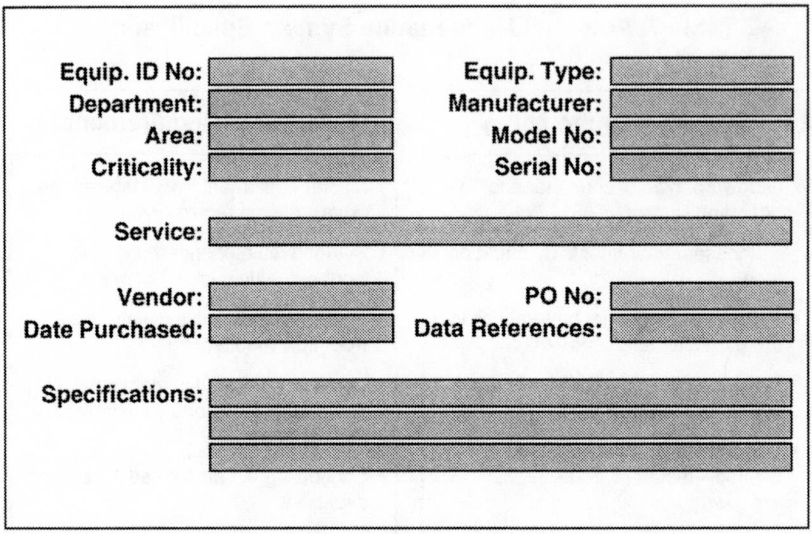

Equip. ID No: [____]    Equip. Type: [____]
Department: [____]    Manufacturer: [____]
Area: [____]    Model No: [____]
Criticality: [____]    Serial No: [____]

Service: [_____]

Vendor: [____]    PO No: [____]
Date Purchased: [____]    Data References: [____]

Specifications: [_____]
[_____]
[_____]

**Figure 5. Simplified Master Equipment List Format**

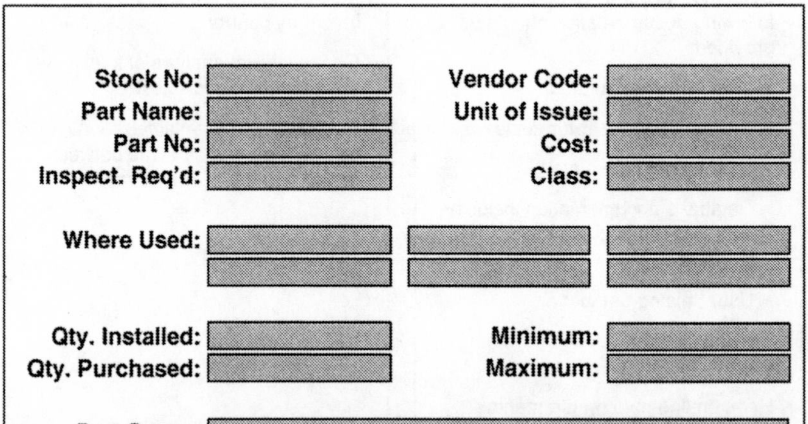

Stock No: [____]    Vendor Code: [____]
Part Name: [____]    Unit of Issue: [____]
Part No: [____]    Cost: [____]
Inspect. Req'd: [____]    Class: [____]

Where Used: [____]  [____]  [____]
[____]  [____]  [____]

Qty. Installed: [____]    Minimum: [____]
Qty. Purchased: [____]    Maximum: [____]

Part Specs: [_____]
[_____]
[_____]

**Figure 6. Simplified Recommended Spare Parts List Format**

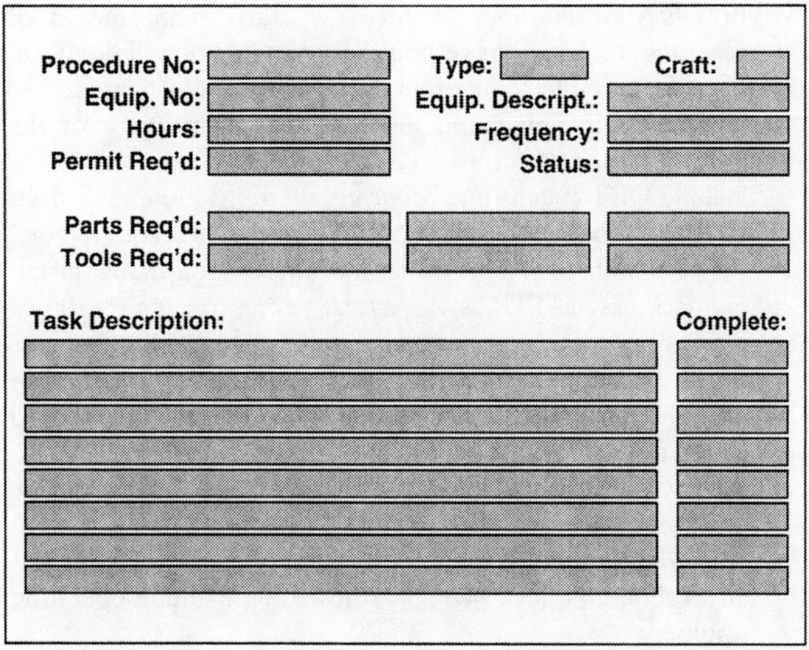

| Procedure No: | | Type: | | Craft: | |
|---|---|---|---|---|---|
| Equip. No: | | Equip. Descript.: | | | |
| Hours: | | Frequency: | | | |
| Permit Req'd: | | Status: | | | |

Parts Req'd: 

Tools Req'd: 

Task Description:                                                              Complete:

**Figure 7. Simplified Preventive Maintenance Procedure Format**

preventive maintenance plan may include predictive maintenance tasks for ease of managing the data. Figure 7 details the
data structure for a simple preventive maintenance database.

6. Define procedures and assign responsibilities to ensure that
the system of maintenance is kept up-to-date and continually
improved. A system owner or "champion" should accept
responsibility for database maintenance, training of new
people, system administration, and software vendor liaison.
The champion can also document system policies and procedures, and police adherence to them.

7. Estimate resource requirements for the PM plan in terms of
hours of each skill required to execute individual tasks.
Additional, dedicated resources or overtime may be required
to perform the tasks when the PM program is first initiated

or when autonomous maintenance starts. The amount of resources required for responsive maintenance will diminish, though, as the benefits of increased PM and PdM surface.

8. Implement the plan and measure the performance of the process itself and results from the process. Typical measures include OEE, mean time between failure (MTBF), and mean time to repair (MTTR). MTBF is the average interval between failures of a particular machine or a particular group of machines. MTTR is the average time to repair a failed piece of equipment or equipment group. Sample process measures are the percent of PM jobs accomplished on schedule and the percent of maintenance labor-hours devoted to planned maintenance.

9. Review the PM and PdM databases regularly and optimize the systems according to operating experience. Items such as scheduling intervals, redundant tasks, and actual PM procedures should be reviewed and adjusted based upon operating results.

Although the above recommended approach is straightforward, significant effort is required to execute the plan. Most companies perform many of the above steps in one form or another, but efforts often bog down due to lack of adequate resources. The above approach is simple, has proven successful for hundreds of companies, and generates tremendous bottom-line results. Not surprisingly, many of the best managed companies in North America have the best maintenance systems. They have made a commitment to planned maintenance systems that work and that produce financial benefits.

One key cultural issue must be recognized and addressed when transitioning to a planned system of maintenance. In reactive environments, the maintenance department has been evaluated based on its ability to respond to equipment breakdowns and restore the equipment to operation as quickly as possible. Management applauded and recognized supervisors and their crews for successfully responding to emergency situations and

minimizing production stoppages. Implementing planned maintenance as part of TPM gradually helps eliminate emergency
incidents. But for this to happen, management must begin singing
the praises of people whose equipment never fails. In the past,
such people went unnoticed, while those whose machines mal-
functioned received kudos for bringing it back on line.
Management must reward the behavior and results it seeks to
promote. The real value of a maintenance department is in pre-
venting failures, not in responding to them. More valuable
measures of success are demonstrated by attainment of the
concept of zero and minimizing total life cycle costs of equipment.

The intent of the Japan Institute of Plant Maintenance is to recognize crisis prevention rather than crisis recovery. JIPM has dealt
effectively with this cultural issue through the PM Prize. As mentioned earlier, there is no such universally accepted award
available in North America. Some commercially motivated
attempts by service suppliers do provide recognition for maintenance or reliability excellence. Organizations which have
established awards include *Plant Engineering* magazine and A. T.
Kearney ("Best of the Best" award), *Maintenance Technology*
magazine (annual best plant awards), and CSI, a marketer of predictive maintenance tools (predictive maintenance awards). In
addition, some companies offer internal awards to plants for
achieving a level of planned maintenance excellence, such as Ford's
Preventive Maintenance Excellence Award or DuPont's
Maintenance Excellence Recognition Award.

## Step Ten: Provide Training to Improve Operator and Maintenance Skills

Training inevitably plays a major role in any improvement
process. The continual investment in employees by upgrading their
skills and capabilities is as critical as investing in plant equipment.
People are an organization's most important asset. Their importance is recognized and promoted by the TPM process.

In the North American TPM process, the traditional roles of the production operator and maintenance craftsperson are being reinvented. Operators are accepting greater responsibility for the health and performance of the equipment as they take on certain maintenance tasks that historically were performed by maintenance craftspeople. The craftspeople, in turn, are relinquishing many routine maintenance tasks such as checking, adjusting, and lubricating the equipment. Their efforts are increasingly allocated to higher value-added activities. Rather than simply being repairmen, they now are problem-solvers performing the highly skilled analytical tasks of root cause analysis, reliability centered maintenance, and equipment redesign. These changes in responsibilities for operators and craftspeople have required a new emphasis on both basic and advanced technical training.

Besides the additional technical skills development, behavior modification and process training is facilitating the change in historical work practices. This type of training usually focuses on the change process and covers such subjects as group dynamics, communications workshops, single-point lessons, and the use of disciplined systems and procedures. Typical subject matter for these classes is as follows:

### Group Dynamics

- Steps to forming small groups
- Soliciting input on goals and improvement processes
- Using collective talents of the group
- Designing a meeting format and agenda
- Meeting management
- Building teamwork, pride, and camaraderie

### Communications Workshops

- Listening for ideas
- Role playing and role reversal
- Providing positive feedback
- Giving opinions without offending others

Single-Point Lessons

- Designing the format and content of single-point lessons
- Using visuals to present ideas
- Using examples from the workplace to reinforce ideas
- Developing procedures to document, track, and administer single-point lessons

Maintenance Systems

- The value of data
- The importance of discipline or adherence to procedures
- The right systems for the job
- Proper use of systems—procedures, work flow, data collection, reporting, and control

Various formats or tools can be used to train or transfer skills to the workforce. In many cases, the needed new skills already exist in the organization. That knowledge or experience simply needs to be dispersed. The following are key methods of transferring skills.

## Single-Point Lessons

One of the most powerful tools for transferring skills is the single-point lesson. This teaching technique helps people learn a specific skill or concept in a short period of time through extensive use of visual images. The skill being taught is typically presented, demonstrated, discussed, reinforced, practiced, and documented in thirty minutes or less. Single-point lessons are especially effective in transferring the technical skills required for a production operator to assume minor maintenance responsibilities.

Most North American plants and facilities have been using single-point lessons for years under different names. A company's safety program is a clear example. Weekly safety meetings, led by supervisors or subject-matter experts, have educated employees in proper procedures for using ladders, lifting heavy weights, and locking out machinery. These sessions are typically performed in a small group environment.

A maintenance craftsperson with good technical and communication skills is capable of developing and presenting a series of single-point lessons for operators or less experienced craftspeople. Natural topics might include proper use of tools such as torque wrenches or grease guns. Or they might address issues related to specific plant processes or equipment. The maintenance engineer also can join these activities by providing single-point lessons to maintenance personnel about investigating and trending equipment histories, or reading vibration spectra. Operators can teach each other specific skills using single-point lessons.

Every plant should develop and set priorities for topics that can be handled by single-point lessons. The identification of potential topics should be accomplished by canvassing workers for ideas and areas of need. Initially, each worker might be requested to develop a list of activities and skills that are required to perform his standard job function. This information can be compiled in small group meetings and consolidated by the group leader into a single document representing the needs of the group. Small, focused topics then can be selected and assigned to individuals for development of single-point lessons.

Besides handling technical issues, single-point lessons can focus on the process of change. Sample topics might include: how to submit an improvement idea, handling constructive disagreement, measuring results, and team problem solving. Single-point lessons also can teach specific, system related issues: completing a work request, plotting OEE data, or developing and using lubrication pictorials. Although a central organization should oversee the administration of single-point lessons, their actual development and delivery should be handled by individual small work groups and shared with the rest of the plant.

### Workshops

Although single-point lessons can be used to transfer behavioral modification skills, other methods, because they are more subtle or sophisticated, may be more effective. A more common method to introduce behavioral skills is through workshops that take place in a formal classroom setting, lasting from two to eight hours. Ideally, they provide a simulated environment modeled after the plant workplace, and enable participants to develop skills through role playing or other exercises. Due to their potential complexity, these workshops are best taught by professional trainers.

Communications workshops are a good example of how behavior can be modified. They focus on how to communicate ideas, issues, problems, and situations in a constructive manner that respects all viewpoints of the organization. The lesson plan usually calls for presentation of communication theories followed by role playing in which the participants practice use of the new techniques. Often, participants reverse roles in order to comprehend another's viewpoint. For example, a craftsperson may adopt the role of a maintenance manager in disciplining an individual for poor performance, while the role of the individual being disciplined may be acted out by a supervisor or even the plant manager. These role-playing sessions can have a major impact in promoting the teamwork and cooperation necessary for effective employee involvement and empowerment.

If management consistently reinforces skills learned in the workshops, plants can undergo a major, positive change in attitude. One plant in the steel industry needed to confront serious attitudinal problems resulting from a 20 percent downsizing of the plant population. A plant survey on attitudes revealed a 78 percent unfavorable rating on job satisfaction resulting from fears, doubts, and uncertainties about people's jobs. Following three months of communications workshops, the rating reversed itself to 63 percent favorable.

The following is a sampling of behavioral topics related to TPM that can be taught effectively in a workshop environment:

- Effective small group activities
- Creative decision making
- Managing conflict
- Interpersonal communication skills
- Problem-solving techniques

Workshops also can be used productively for non-behavioral subjects. Some subjects may be very complex and too large or general to deal with solely through single-point lessons. Examples are topics such as: failure mode and effects analysis, complex TPM measurables, and organization of a comprehensive PM program. In other instances there may be value in tying together a series of single-point lessons and presenting them on a unified basis in a workshop. Then they can be reinforced singly in the field.

### One-on-One Coaching

After completing a workshop, an initial groundswell of enthusiasm and euphoria is common as participants seek to change their work environment. Unfortunately, this emotion normally can not be sustained and employees revert to their old work habits. Outside stimuli, consistently reinforced by management, is an ideal way to perpetuate lasting change and specifically reinforce what was learned in the workshop. Perhaps the most effective form is one-on-one coaching provided by management, human resource representatives, or consultants. This can be a time-consuming and costly approach, but one that brings about true behavioral change. The aim is to institutionalize desired behavior through constant reminders and constructive feedback of what is or is not acceptable. The objective is to help employees take theoretical skills out of the classroom and apply them to their real-world environment.

### Video Training Aids

Video technology is inexpensive today and can be an invaluable training tool. Although many off-the-shelf products are available, internal production of training materials has the advantage of providing employees with increased ownership over the educational process. The videotaping of equipment maintenance procedures, ranging from minor checks to complete overhauls, can be performed with in-house resources at low cost. These videotapes also

have the advantage of addressing plant-specific equipment or procedures, although they may lack the overall quality of generic tapes
that are professionally developed. Some companies are using videos
as a foundation of their training efforts. A plant in the chemical
industry, for example, has more than 1800 hours of videotape on
maintenance tasks. Video training offers advantages over books
because of its ability to provide constant visual reinforcement of the
tasks being performed. The best tapes use a step-by-step approach
to show how a task, such as an engine rebuild, is performed. This
provides the viewer with an excellent feel for the difficulty and pre-
cision required at each step. When the time comes to actually
rebuild an engine, the worker can replay certain portions of the
tape to review the techniques, time, and tools required.

Taping of workshops or management presentations can also
augment technical training efforts. The taping lets individuals who
were unable to attend the workshops learn the concepts by
viewing the tapes at their leisure. Small group activities also are
benefited greatly if they have easy access to video equipment and
are encouraged to use it.

## Skill Certification

Many organizations provide a mechanism to certify the proficiency of their employees. Skills certification benefits companies
by ensuring that jobs are more likely to be performed in a safe and
high quality manner. Moreover, as government regulations
increase, organizations such as OSHA are placing greater burdens
on companies to prove, not only that they have provided adequate
training, but that employees have learned from it and are competent in their jobs. Although some unions resist testing of their
members, that resistance is based on their fear that management
will use the tests to rid themselves of unwanted employees.
Management must build rapport with these union groups, so that
they understand that the intent of testing is to provide the additional support needed to make every worker safe and productive
in his position.

Most individuals are motivated to become certified as part of their basic human nature to be recognized. The skills they learn often can be used outside the work site. Should they become, in a worst case scenario, the victims of a workforce reduction, the certification of their skill levels makes them more employable to other companies. People's natural motivation to improve can be augmented by providing increased compensation for the use of those skills. Pay for knowledge and performance is becoming a more prevalent part of negotiated contracts.

Precedents exist in North America for certification of many professions. Public accountants, professional engineers, lawyers, doctors, and some union crafts must be certified on competency in their respective fields. Some classifications such as airline pilots require recertification at specified intervals.

Certification can be a subjective, simple acknowledgment of attendance at a class, or it can be quantitatively based on passing comprehensive, detailed tests. One company in the contract maintenance business uses a formal certification program that involves tests and on-the-job follow-up. A plastic card resembling a credit card documents the certified proficiency levels of employees in more than twenty skill areas such as pipefitter, electrician, millwright, carpenter, sheet metal, and welding. Individuals study at home and practice the skills on the job. Once skills are mastered, employee records and the plastic card are updated to indicate certification in the new skill. Periodic recertification is also being considered as a part of the program in the future. Many craftspeople are certified in ten or more skills, providing increased job security for themselves and greater flexibility to the company.

Certification should be an integral part of the TPM process, and should complement any other certification process already in use at the plant. Recommended types of certification for the TPM process include:

- Certified TPM Instructor
- Certified Small Group Leader / Facilitator
- Certified Mechanic on particular equipment items
- Certified Operator for Lubrication
- Certified Autonomous Work Group

Many companies already have a formal training organization devoted to improving and certifying employee skills. These departments can help implement step ten of the TPM process, but accountability for the effort must lie with line management.

## Step Eleven: Develop an Early Equipment Management Program

Good equipment management techniques improve the use of capital assets and extend their life cycle. The objective is to maximize a company's total investment in equipment. This is accomplished by ensuring that individuals and groups understand their role in equipment management, so that they know how their activities impact the total life cycle of the equipment. Traditionally, the equipment management function is divided into the following phases:

- *Specification.* Specification is the process for identifying the functions and requirements of proposed equipment. Although only a small percentage of the life cycle cost is expended during the specification phase, it has a major impact on total life costs of the equipment. Operating efficiencies, future maintenance requirements, and utility usage are largely determined by the equipment specification.
- *Procurement.* Procurement matches the company's needs, as defined by the specifications, with the product of an internal or external supplier. Procurement includes bid solicitation, bid analysis, vendor negotiation, and contract for purchase.
- *Startup or Commissioning.* This is the initial phase of equipment operation and lasts until equipment reaches stable operation. It bridges the gap between initial equipment installation and normal operation.
- *Operation.* Operation is the activity associated with stable, long-term supervision of the equipment including production, maintenance, and rebuild. The operation phase is where value is generated by the machine to the organization.
- *Disposal.* Disposal is the scrapping of out-of-date, deteriorated, or unneeded equipment. The elimination of equipment is handled in an environmentally sound manner.

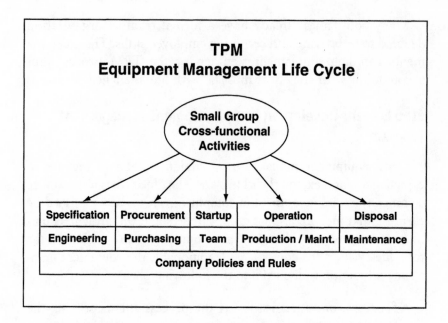

**Figure 8. TPM Equipment Management Life Cycle**

Typically, each phase of equipment management has been managed independently of the others. Production, marketing, or another function specifies equipment needs and passes the request over the wall to engineering. Engineering designs equipment specifications and, in turn, tosses the package over the wall to purchasing. Purchasing then completes the vendor selection, negotiations, and contract terms and throws the results over to a launch team or maintenance. This basic process is repeated because each department or function works independently or in isolation. Since each department only sees their part of the puzzle, innumerable problems arise when the equipment is placed in operation. Production often discovers that the equipment does not meet their requirements, or maintenance finds that parts are not standardized with other equipment or are not readily available. The typical life-cycle process for equipment is depicted in Table 8.

## Table 8. Typical Phases of Equipment Management

| Phase | Responsibility | Costs | Analytical Effort |
|-------|----------------|-------|-------------------|
| Specification | Management and engineering | Costs are minimal, typically less than 5 percent of total life-cycle cost. However, this is the phase where the majority of the life-cycle cost is defined. Poor specification and design leads to higher total life-cycle costs. | High effort. Most of the technical effort spent on the equipment is in the specification phase. Too much effort is spent on controlling the purchase cost and not enough on controlling the operational cost. |
| Procurement | Purchasing with engineering reserving veto power | Costs can appear to be high, but are typically only a small percentage of the operating cost. | Most effort is spent on contract terms and vendor prices. Little effort is spent on ensuring continuing vendor support and incentive-based performance guarantees. |
| Startup | Launch team consisting of representatives from engineering, production, and maintenance, with assistance by the vendor if dictated by the contract for purchase | Costs can be relatively high. Most of the launch cost is typically due to delays in the startup schedule representing lost opportunity when production is delayed. | This the end of engineering involvement. Engineering and the vendor are motivated to rush through the effort to get to the next project. Most analytical effort is spent on redesigns or fixes to original design errors. The fixes are typically tactical and not strategic. |
| Operation | Production and maintenance | Costs are by far the largest of any phase, typically as high as 80 percent of the total life-cycle cost. These costs are not analyzed or controlled as equipment performance tends to steadily decline. | Little or no analytical resource is available. Engineering is working on projects, maintenance is fighting fires, and production is pressed for schedule compliance. |
| Disposal | Maintenance | Costs in terms of lingering liabilities can be enormous. Costs can be minimal if sufficient up-front engineering is performed. | Little or no analytical work or planning is performed unless there are hazards associated with disposal. |

New emphasis has been placed on equipment management in strategies such as concurrent or simultaneous engineering. These efforts recognize that groups cannot perform their functions in a vacuum. Various functions such as production and maintenance must work concurrently with engineering to ensure optimal design and performance of equipment.

The TPM process integrates these new philosophies of equipment management through the use of employee empowerment and small group activities at every level of the organization. Some American companies, as reflected in General Motors' Saturn project and Chrysler's LH series project, have experimented successfully with these concepts. In both cases, plant floor workers were brought into the project during the design phase, and worked directly with design engineers and equipment suppliers to ensure a manufacturing process that was both easy to operate and easy to maintain.

During equipment specification and procurement, TPM focuses on lowering total life-cycle cost through the use of maintenance prevention design, design for operability, and design for maintainability. To effect this concept, design engineering identifies their own small group activities and invites production and maintenance personnel to participate in the specification and actual selection of equipment. The same small group determines equipment layout design focusing on operability, maintainability and optimum material flow. Once the equipment vendors are selected, they become de facto members of the small groups. The vendor's involvement continues beyond the startup phase and into the operation phase. The small groups also manage the startup phase including planning, scheduling, and equipment checks. Operations and maintenance participation in the startup provides numerous side benefits, since it becomes an excellent training ground for operation and maintenance of the equipment. After the startup phase, the design engineers become less involved in the equipment management process and turn leadership of the small groups over to production and maintenance personnel. Once the useful life of the equipment is expended, the small group becomes responsible for its disposal.

Small group activity in overall equipment management is practiced in Japan at all of the PM-Prize-winning plants. The difference in Japan is that the equipment supplier is much more likely to be an internal rather than an external supplier. For example, in the Toyota group of companies, most of the equipment that is used in the automobile assembly plants is developed in-house or procured from another Toyota company. This promotes a greater partnership with all of the groups associated with the equipment life cycle. This type of partnership can be duplicated in North America. Rather than the confrontational approach that normally exists in many customer/supplier relationships, these new relationships must be founded on trust and teamwork.

Although small groups have autonomy in managing their equipment, they are still accountable for operating within the bounds of company policies and rules. Individual departments within the plant must implement checks and balances to ensure that policies and rules are followed.

The quality of equipment management by small group activities depends on the effective and efficient use of data and information as decision support tools. Data on equipment operation, performance, and productivity must be communicated to the small groups in a format that is understood easily. An effective internal communication device is a well-designed activity board. The activity board should detail current performance, trends, and improvement activities to provide understanding and motivation. In addition, equipment activity board data on modifications, failure analysis, PM records, and autonomous maintenance improvements should flow back to design engineering and the equipment vendors for continual improvements on next generation designs.

Japanese factories post activity boards for each significant plant area and for each small group. The boards are frequently quite large, as much as 10 feet high by 20 feet long. Specific areas of the boards are sectioned off to provide:

- information on equipment performance (OEE and its components)
- the latest single-point lessons

- all of the suggestions received from employees along with their status
- a list of outstanding equipment concerns or issues
- plans for the future
- progress on current activities
- reports on significant improvements

Many of the boards are integrated with product quality reporting and include the use of statistical process control (SPC) charts. Liberal use of pictures and drawings make the activity boards readable and easy to understand. Even an individual who does not know Japanese can understand and evaluate equipment performance trends and improvement. The use of activity boards fits well with the concept of a "visual factory."

## Step Twelve: Perfect TPM Implementation and Raise TPM Levels

TPM benefits are realized or recognized through celebrations. North American companies generally are comfortable celebrating or rewarding upper management for their successes. Praise, bonuses, stock options, and generous fringe benefits are part of the package. Sales meetings in exotic locations are awarded to successful sales personnel who meet their quota. But the celebrations fizzle at middle management and lower levels. Plant floor personnel usually only receive encouraging words and small tokens of appreciation from their direct managers. Upper management's superficial efforts at recognizing plant floor achievements indicate their lack of understanding of how to reinforce continuous improvement processes.

### Why Do We Celebrate?

It is human nature to celebrate the achievement of goals. Events such as birthdays, anniversaries, and graduations are meaningful milestones in people's lives. By highlighting accomplishments in the workplace, management has an opportunity to intensify employees' sense of worth and loyalty to the company. In addition, celebration and reward structures can help embed new processes or methods and motivate efforts toward increasingly higher performance levels.

Celebrations let people feel good about their accomplishments. Continuous improvement is hard work, and people's enthusiasm must be recharged periodically. Celebrations symbolize the attainment of crucial milestones and provide meaning to people's work efforts. People work to earn money and recognition. Setting appropriate goals and rewards can solidify teamwork and promote cooperation.

The Japanese celebrate the successes of their plants with great fanfare and enthusiasm. Since they view the events as an investment in their company and people, they deliberately include all levels of the organization. Planned months in advance, the plant is shut down for the day of the ceremony. The company's highest officials, as well as local government officials and the media, are in attendance. Workers and their families participate in a party-like atmosphere including music, catered meals, and commemorative gifts. In one celebration held by a Japanese-owned facility in California, the plant gave a car to the city for its support. This was good business, since it left both the city and company employees feeling pleased about their role in bringing about improvements.

Planning is critical to the success of celebrations. One plant recently missed a major opportunity to build enthusiasm for its improvement efforts. Having earned a company-sponsored quality award, they failed to build additional support for the process through an appropriate celebration. Although the award was presented by a company official with corporate staff responsibility for quality, the event took only 30 minutes and consisted of a plaque being presented to the plant manager. The ceremony was broadcast on the plant public address system and employees were given a coupon good for a free cafeteria lunch, but the remote event meant little to the plant floor worker.

### What Defines Success?

Success in our improvement efforts should be defined by the goals established in step four of the TPM process. If these goals are accomplished, then celebration is in order. TPM is a multi-year commitment, and the Japanese work diligently for years in pursuit of their TPM objectives. North American culture is more short-sighted and people want to see bottom-line signs of progress quickly. Therefore, North American companies must be prepared to celebrate critical short-term milestones. Normal milestones should be achieved in less than 12 months, if reasonable efforts are expended. The milestones should reflect completion of TPM phases and improvements in plant performance. Results should be as quantitative as possible, so that little room exists for interpretation of the measures. The sample TPM deployment plan included in the appendix of this book includes five major milestones for which celebration is in order. They include:

- formal kickoff for the process
- achieve OEE targets on critical equipment
- full autonomous maintenance implementation
- planned maintenance system implementation
- realization of TPM benefits and challenges for new targets

### How Do We Celebrate?

Celebrations can take many forms, but their purpose is to allow employees to derive satisfaction from their work efforts and accomplishments, while simultaneously setting new challenges. Ceremonies that recognize one group of an organization at the expense of another do more harm than good. Celebrations must specifically recognize all parties that participated in the process. The following is a list of common attributes of the most successful celebrations, Japanese or American:

- The celebration is moderated by an accomplished presenter who is recognized and respected by all participants.

- Senior-level management (representing corporate and plant groups) attends, and endorses the process through active participation.
- Plant floor employees present their accomplishments. The professionalism of their presentations is secondary to the pride and enthusiasm they exhibit in their accomplishments.
- The event is widely publicized through company newsletters, local newspapers, and other appropriate media.
- Suppliers, customers, and community leaders join in the celebration to recognize their own contributions as well the achievements of the plant.
- Symbols of the event (belt buckles, jackets, baseball caps, or pocket knives with commemorative markings) are distributed to all participants.
- Special awards (monuments, plaques, flags, or banners) are distributed to individuals, groups, or plant representatives.

A key part of the event is to challenge participants to even higher levels of performance. If orchestrated correctly, organizational energy can be harnessed and directed to critical, future plant needs. If the organization is not immediately challenged, an emotional letdown is likely. Several companies have seen plants receive a company sponsored or nationally recognized award, and then watched performance drop significantly the following year. The problem is not unlike that faced by teams winning the Super Bowl or the World Series. Consecutive championships are rare. In locker room celebrations, managers praise their players for reaching their goal while also exhorting them to greater efforts the next year. In sports, as in business, the best must continue to improve at a rate faster than that of their competition.

# 5
# The Seven Levels of
# Autonomous Maintenance

Autonomous maintenance is considered by many people to be the simple transfer of maintenance tasks to production operators. This is a gross simplification of the process. Under autonomous maintenance, production operators assume increased responsibility for the maintenance of their equipment as they take on tasks traditionally reserved for maintenance personnel. But this involves much more than a simple transfer of responsibilities. The seven steps of autonomous maintenance present an extremely organized approach for ensuring optimal equipment performance. Key elements of the approach focus on improving equipment cleanliness, developing cleaning and lubrication standards, developing inspection procedures, organizing work areas, and continuously improving the work process.

Autonomous maintenance has a drastic impact on the traditional approach to equipment management. Tasks are designed, not only to maintain equipment, but to establish a more conducive atmosphere for improving equipment performance. The intent is to increase production operators' awareness of their equipment and physical environment. Barriers that limit their ability to observe and affect equipment performance are systematically removed. The result is that operators take increased interest in their areas of responsibility.

The seven levels of autonomous maintenance include the following:

1. Initial cleaning
2. Preventive cleaning measures
3. Development of cleaning and lubrication standards
4. General inspection
5. Autonomous inspection
6. Process discipline
7. Independent autonomous maintenance

Each of the above levels builds upon the previous one in establishing new standards for equipment performance. The specific activities associated with each step enable incremental improvements in the overall capabilities and reliability of equipment. Complete autonomous maintenance facilitates a cultural change in the operation, as teamwork, cooperation, and communication are expanded between maintenance and production departments.

## Initial Cleaning

The purpose of initial cleaning is threefold. First, small work groups are able to join together in accomplishing a common goal, the cleaning of a particular machine or process. Second, it promotes a better understanding of, and familiarity with, the machine or process area. Third, the actual machine cleaning regularly uncovers hidden defects that, when corrected, have a positive effect on equipment performance.

The activities associated with initial cleaning are typically performed by members of the small groups as part of initial TPM training. In designating what cleaning tasks are of most value, the experiences of a qualified TPM trainer can be invaluable. The cleaning is performed as a group activity. Although individual tasks are assigned, the small group retains total control over the project. The production operator who is regularly responsible for the machine must be a part of the cleaning team if the group is to achieve the full benefits of the activity. If necessary, prior to initiating the cleaning, all team members should receive training in safety procedures associated with the chosen equipment. Lock out, work permit, confined space entry, and hazardous material handling are a portion of the requirements with which individuals must be familiar.

Initial cleaning is not intended to be an overhaul or turnaround of the equipment or process area. The focus is to increase understanding of the equipment through the cleaning process. If one were to perform initial cleaning on an automobile engine, key tasks would include steam cleaning the engine exterior, retorquing head-gasket bolts, and possibly replacing the fan belt and doing a compression check. But one would not remove the head, hone the cylinder walls, or replace the crankshaft bearings.

The following steps are guidelines for small groups in performing initial cleaning:

- Perform all activities necessary to shut down, isolate, and make the equipment or process area totally safe.
- Obtain copies of equipment drawings, documentation, histories, and other relevant information. If drawings do not exist, prepare sketches of the equipment or scan photographs for use in documenting lube points, adjustment points, and process check points. This documentation is used in successive levels of autonomous maintenance to develop standards for lubrication and autonomous inspections.
- Document initial condition of the equipment through photographs. Prepare forms for documenting equipment defects and tags for marking items needing further inspection.

- Segment portions of the machine or process area and plan how to clean the machine or area with maximum efficiency and effectiveness.
- Obtain hand tools, rags, brushes, solvents, mops, brooms, scrapers and any other tools required to perform the cleaning tasks.
- Clean each machine segment in a methodical manner. Remember that the goal is to put the machine back into an as-new condition, to pass a "white glove" test.
- Remove all dirt, grime, dust, grease, oil, sludge, chips, trash, and excess materials. Note any equipment abnormalities such as broken switches, bent guards, missing bolts, and leaks. Cleaning is also inspection. Take the time needed to do a thorough and complete job. Speed is not nearly as important as understanding and working together as a team.
- Tag and document all equipment abnormalities. Address easily corrected abnormalities immediately, and write work requests for others.
- Retorque all bolts including hold-down, fastener, adjustment, and structural bolts. Mark all bolts by painting a stripe across both the stud head and the bolt to indicate the relative positions of both when properly torqued. Any future slippage or loosening of the bolt then can be noted easily as the marks will no longer line up.
- Repaint areas if necessary according to predetermined specifications. The purpose of repainting is not just to prevent corrosion, but to provide a surface that can be examined easily for cleanliness. Color-code piping, utilities, and guards for ease of observation.
- Note and mark all lubrication points. Document the points on a lubrication chart and mark the point physically on the machine. Color coding can be performed by painting a small colored circle in close proximity to the lubrication point. Some plants use a plastic colored "sticker" to mark the position and lubricant type instead of a paint circle. The color of

the circle designates the type of lubricant. Lubricant containers also can be color coded by painting the container the same color as the lubrication point circles.

- Note and mark all adjustment points, gauges, and utility connections, as well as material entry and exit points. This helps ensure that all small group members are totally familiar with the machine or process area.
- Photograph the clean machine or process area and compare with a "before" photograph to verify progress.
- Formally turn the equipment or process area back to production for startup and operation. Have the small group participate in the setup and startup activities for greater understanding of equipment operation.

The time required to complete the above steps may exceed available time for a given shutdown period. It may be necessary to schedule the above steps over several shutdown periods to accommodate operating requirements.

Dozens of equipment abnormalities or improvement suggestions may result from the initial cleaning activities on a single machine. Many of the equipment issues will be fixed or improved immediately during the initial cleaning activities. Others will be backlogged as work requests to be performed by skilled trades or external contractors.

Depending on existing equipment conditions, initial cleaning activities may require a major commitment of time and resouces. Most companies underestimate the size of the commitment. Once they recognize the extent of resources required, they either cut back on the amount of equipment to be included or perform only superficial cleaning. Some Japanese companies invest as much as 160 hours per plant employee, not just maintenance workers, on this initial cleaning activity. The labor hours usually are performed on an overtime basis. Much of the funding for the effort comes from the plant training budget. The rationale is that employees receive significant training benefits in performing the cleaning.

As with all investments, potential benefits and risks must be evaluated. The benefits associated with autonomous maintenance can be difficult to estimate, so some general guidelines are in order. First, the overall equipment effectiveness of plant processes must be known, so that an OEE measure can be correlated with financial results. This allows projections of financial gains from improving the OEE. The next step is to estimate the increase in OEE that can be realized through the initial cleaning portion of autonomous maintenance. This is highly dependent on individual production processes. Normally if the current OEE is 60 percent or below, initial cleaning can increase it by 20 or more percentage points. If the OEE is above 60 percent, the increase typically will be half the difference between the OEE and 100 percent. For example, initial cleaning should increase a 70 percent OEE to 85 percent or an 80 percent OEE to 90 percent.

A "real world" example of a food processing plant can help illustrate the process. The plant had several bottling lines where bottles of juice were filled, capped, labeled, and packaged. The OEE of each line was controlled or limited by one machine, the filler. A quick study showed that the average OEE for the lines was approximately 55 percent. The plant was running at capacity, but could not meet market demands. The annual sales volume of the plant was $125 million, and the plant controller had calculated that the profit margin on each incremental case produced by the plant would be 32 percent without additional fixed costs. Using the guidelines stated earlier, initial cleaning could increase OEE by 15 to 20 percentage points. Using the conservative 15 percent projection, the plant OEE could be increased to 70 percent through initial cleaning. The impact on plant sales volume is seen in the following formula:

$$\text{volume at 70\% OEE} = (70\% \text{ OEE} \div 55\% \text{ OEE}) \times \$125 \text{ million}$$
$$= \$159 \text{ million}$$

The incremental volume would be $34 million. At a 32 percent profit margin on the additional production, the bottom line profit increase for the plant is $10.9 million. This was more than enough to finance the initial cleaning efforts.

Subsequent levels of autonomous maintenance solidify and institutionalize benefits gained in the initial cleaning process. Each level is designed to support productivity without additional extraordinary efforts such as those required in the initial cleaning exercise. Although the initial cleaning process has short-term value by itself, long-term effects require successful implementation of other autonomous maintenance activities.

## Preventive Cleaning Measures

Many plants embark periodically on a major cleaning effort. The intent is to impress visiting executives or prepare for plant tours associated with family days. Following the cleaning, the plant quickly reverts to old operating methods and housekeeping deteriorates. Preventive cleaning measures are designed to "engineer" a solution for maintaining cleanliness.

Declines in housekeeping standards result from contamination entering and remaining in the machine or work area. During preventive cleaning measures, sources of contamination are identified, isolated, and controlled. Basically, there are three types of contamination—leaks, process excess, and external environment. Each source of contamination must be correctly diagnosed and dealt with separately.

Initial cleaning activities identify contaminants that reside in the machine or area. Each contaminant type should be identified and documented. Typical contaminants include leaking process fluids, leaking lubricants, dust, corrosion, process scrap, material handling scrap, worker-generated trash, and other external pollutants. Contaminant identification can not always be accomplished during the initial cleanup activities. Many times, due to the volume of contaminant and the years of buildup, the initial cleanup activity can identify only that a contaminant exists. An example is seen in a discrete manufacturing plant that was built a few years ago.

Management was concerned that the plant was not able to match the productivity numbers of its sister plants in Europe, even though the European plants were at least twenty years older. The plant had hundreds of grinding machines. Each machine was equipped with a catch basin, which was loaded with metal shavings, oil, cigarette butts, and candy wrappers. It was impossible to identify whether the oil was cutting oil, hydraulic oil, or another lubricant. When asked why the catch basins were not cleaned in an attempt to increase machine reliability, the tour guide's reply was, "They would just get dirty again." Personnel at this plant failed to understand that clean machines lead to improved equipment performance.

Under their current operating conditions, the plant could not identify either the total list of contaminants, their sources, or their impact on grinder performance. The best method of identifying contaminants in these situations is to clean the machine and then place it back in normal operation. By closely monitoring the buildup of contaminants through inspections, the contaminant can be identified along with its source and rate of contamination.

## Process Leaks

One of the most common forms of machine contamination is process leaks. The simplest method of identifying and correcting process-fluid leaks is to use a leak tag system (see Figure 9). A leak tag normally consists of a two-part form with a "twist tie" mechanism allowing the tag to be affixed in close proximity to the leak. The forms are made readily available to all plant personnel by being placed in convenient locations throughout the plant. The tags are red, yellow, or another bright color, so that they can be spotted easily when affixed to machines or piping. Procedures for personnel to use the leak tag system are as follows:

Locate the leak and identify (if possible) its source, the type of fluid leaking, and the severity of the leak.

Fill out the leak tag form noting the above information as well as other appropriate information such as the name of the requester or date.

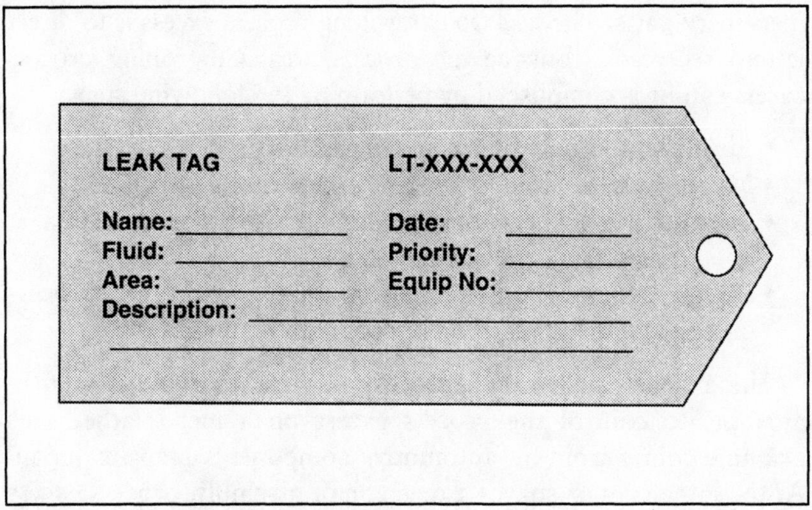

THE SEVEN LEVELS OF AUTONOMOUS MAINTENANCE      101

```
LEAK TAG              LT-XXX-XXX

Name:_____          Date:    _____
Fluid:  _____       Priority: _____
Area:  _____        Equip No: _____
Description: _____
             _____
```

**Figure 9. Typical Leak Tag Form**

Detach the two-part form and affix one portion to the leak or in near proximity.

Send or hand the other part of the form to the organization responsible for backlogging work orders.

Implementation of a simple, easy to use system such as this can save hundreds of thousands of dollars for a plant. Some manufacturing plants have seen a 70 percent to 80 percent reduction in consumption of hydraulic oil after implementation of a leak tag system. Many process plants have had similar successes using the system to identify and repair steam and process air leaks.

### Controlling Process Excess

Several other process-related contaminants can be controlled or eliminated by establishing firm preventive cleaning measures. Many production processes involve cutting or forming process material to make an end product. As part of the process, pieces of material are either scrapped or recycled. This material is "process excess," and typically consists of shavings, chips, process dust, and other scrap material that can be detrimental to bearings and other moving machinery parts. The trick to controlling process excess is to direct it into receptacles outside the process area. Controlling process excess can be accomplished by performing the following steps:

- Identify the source of the process excess.
- Measure the amount of process excess that is generated.
- Measure the direction of movement of the process excess as it is separated from the end product.
- Design a controlling mechanism that absorbs the process excess or redirects it to an appropriate removal vehicle.

These steps can be applied easily. A clear example is seen in attempts to control the process excess on a metal lathe. This example comes from an automotive components plant in Japan. As the lathe cuts or shaves a metal shaft assembly, process excess consisting of metal shavings is mixed with cutting oil. The metal shavings can create havoc with bearings and other rotating equipment and can be hazardous to personnel. The first step is to identify the source of the process excess. In this case, it is where the cutting blade meets the part shaft. The next step is to measure the amount of process excess. This can be accomplished by running the machine for an hour, collecting all the shavings, and weighing them. This should provide a good idea on the rate of process excess production.

The next step requires a bit more ingenuity. The direction in which shavings leave the lathe is identified by where the shavings land. To determine the direction, first draw a circle on the floor around the lathe. The circle should cover a distance slightly more than the farthest a chip has landed from the lathe. Mark eight equal quadrants or pie slices in the circle (see Figure 10). Run the machine for an hour or other appropriate time frame. Pick up all the shavings in each quadrant and weigh them separately. By determining where the majority of shavings landed, you can identify the direction from which they leave the machine.

The final step in the activity is to design a mechanism to control or redirect the metal shavings to an appropriate receptacle. This is

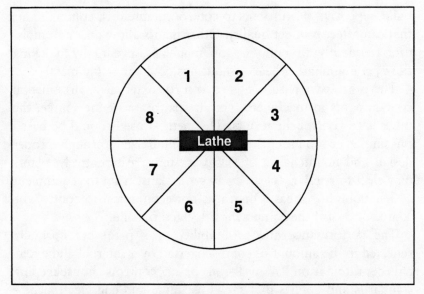

**Figure 10. Measuring the Direction of Movement of Process Excess**

usually done on a trial and error basis, with preliminary designs resulting from data collected from the previous steps. Often shrouds are designed to redirect the process excess to a central location. Initially the shrouds begin as formed cardboard pieces that are taped together. Once a design has been perfected through actual use, permanent pieces are fabricated and retrofitted onto the machine. The design and trial of the shrouds are excellent opportunities to demonstrate the power of small group activities.

### External Environment

External factors can affect machine cleanliness. These typically include dust, people-generated trash, and process-related environmental pollution. Plants usually do a good job of controlling these factors if they directly affect personnel safety or product quality, but the effect on equipment condition is overlooked. Some plants build expensive clean rooms to control minute dust contaminants that can affect product quality. Other plants allow dust and moisture frequently to build up on machines, eventually blocking flows, contaminating bearing housings, and corroding metal.

There are two basic ways to control external environmental contaminants in machinery. The first is to attack the source; the other is to control the results. The method used should be based on simple economics. Dust can be minimized through proper design and maintenance of HVAC systems. Alternatively, plants may elect to regularly clean away settled dust from the equipment and surrounding areas. Often it is not economical to control the source of dust if the equipment is located outside.

The performance and profitability of a plant are normally reflected in the amount of control exerted over internal and external contamination. A well-run plant controls housekeeping standards and applies that same discipline and conscientiousness to all aspects of their business. Poor housekeeping standards are inevitably paralleled by other sloppy business practices. The amount of effort expended by management to control externally generated contaminants such as dust, moisture, and corrosion is usually matched by workers' attempts to reduce contamination that they control. Individual workers are more reluctant to toss candy wrappers and other debris on a clean floor than a dirty one. This is especially true if the worker or his associates have devoted effort and resources to keeping that floor clean.

## Development of Cleaning and Lubrication Standards

The development of cleaning and lubrication standards is a natural progression from the previous two levels of autonomous maintenance. Once a clean work environment is established and steps are taken to prevent deterioration, new, higher standards can be set and documented. The goal is to combine inspections for cleanliness with lubrication checks, so that both activities can be performed together as efficiently as possible. Standards for lubrication and cleanliness also should be developed concurrently.

Small groups should be responsible for developing standards for equipment in their areas. The concept that should guide their work is that cleaning and lubrication are both forms of inspection. Many potential equipment problems can be spotted visually prior to their causing a deterioration in performance. For example, some people establish a standard for the cleanliness and lubrication of their automobiles. In accordance with this self-imposed standard, they periodically open the hood of their car to inspect fluid levels and check or change the lubricant. They also may inspect the engine block for cleanliness, to ensure it is free of spilled oil and road grime. While the hood is up, a quick glance identifies whether the head gasket is leaking and whether there are any loose belts or hoses. These are simple activities that anyone with minor training can perform. The car owner is motivated to meet these standards of cleanliness, so that he can avoid future repair bills. An individual who follows through with this type of inspection is also more likely to exercise greater caution in the operation of his vehicle. He would recognize that it is an acceptable risk to drive a car with a leaking head gasket to the repair shop, but he would not start a car with a broken oil pump.

The format of cleaning and lubrication standards should be similar to that of good preventive maintenance procedures. The exception is that they are developed by and for equipment operators as opposed to maintenance mechanics. Visual images or pictures are excellent for communicating the desired standard. Some standards are developed in the format of a checklist for the production operator, and in other situations single-point lessons depict desired activity. Development of standards requires the following steps:

- Convene small groups under the guidance of a facilitator and create a vision of the equipment's condition as "better than new." Gather and review all relevant material such as manufacturers' manuals, drawings, existing PM check sheets, or historical operational data.
- Describe what each component of the equipment would look like if it were in a "better than new" condition.

- Use existing drawings or develop new ones that visually show the equipment. Label each component of the equipment, and identify each lube point on the picture. Refer to manufacturer or vendor information as appropriate.
- For each component, document the "better than new" condition using terms such as: free of all oil, painted, free of all dust buildup, and free of process excess.
- Establish and document the frequency of cleaning or inspection required to maintain this "better than new" condition.
- For each lube point, document the following:

  ➤ lubricant required
  ➤ reservoir capacity
  ➤ filter requirements
  ➤ frequency of checks
  ➤ frequency of sampling
  ➤ frequency of change
  ➤ safety considerations

- All machine lube points should be physically marked using color codes corresponding to the type of lubricant to be used at that lube point.

The development of these standards provides both tangible and intangible benefits to the plant. First, envisioning the "better than new" environment is a necessary step to making it happen. Second, the documentation process enables each member of the small group to learn more about the design and operation of the machinery. It is common for the small groups to identify points that have never been lubricated or components that have never been cleaned. When these items are pinpointed, they are taken care of immediately, often solving chronic equipment problems. Third, the small groups are further solidified as true teams. Rather than viewing themselves as temporary groups formed to address an immediate issue, they perceive their role as having long lasting, positive effects on the operation of equipment.

## General Inspection

Cleaning and lubrication comprise the bulk of routine inspections needed for most equipment. Additional inspection and adjustment can be grouped into an all-inclusive category called general inspection. These activities include bolt torquing or tightening, minor calibrations, adjustments, replacement of wear parts, and other process-related visual, temperature, pressure, or flow checks. General inspection also includes more detailed inspections on subsystems such as hydraulic, pneumatic, and electrical subsystems.

As was done with the cleaning and lubrication standards, small groups should accept responsibility for the development of general inspection standards. The plant maintenance mechanics possess ideal skills for this process, but production and engineering also should take part. The following tasks are recommended for small groups in developing the remaining general inspection standards:

- Collect all available equipment data including preventive and predictive maintenance procedures, historical operational data, historical failure data, vendor/manufacturers' recommendations, and all design drawings/specifications.
- Review existing preventive maintenance, predictive maintenance, and inspection procedures for accuracy and completeness. Modify the standards and procedures as required to address current needs and update on an ongoing basis.
- Review all equipment failures and isolate their root causes. Failure review and analysis should be an on-going process following each equipment failure. The activity called for here ensures that inspection standards include checks or measures addressing the root causes of previous failures.
- Review manufacturers' and vendors' recommended checks and maintenance procedures. Contact the vendor or manufacturer to determine if there is information/bulletins that should be included in the inspection standards. Review with the vendor and manufacturer the plant's operational and

maintenance experience with the equipment. Solicit their input regarding changes to proposed inspection standards.

- Document the general inspection standards in a format similar to that used for the lubrication and cleaning standards. Use drawings, photographs, hand-drawn pictures, and other pictorial references to visualize the inspection standard.
- Categorize all inspection procedures into those that can be performed presently by production operators, those that can be performed by production operators with training, and those that should be performed by craftspeople.
- Develop check sheets that group sets of inspection by the following categories:

  ➤ the function or craftsperson performing the inspection
  ➤ whether the equipment must be operational or shut down while the inspection is being performed
  ➤ whether disassembly is required
  ➤ ease of performance—in isolation or as part of a combined inspection

- Identify all training required to educate production operators in the safe performance of designated tasks. Use maintenance mechanics to develop supplemental training materials. Pay special attention to defining specifics as to what operators must look for in inspections and how equipment performance is impacted. As operators' understanding of their equipment increases, they will be more attentive to abnormalities and can help design more effective inspection procedures.

One purpose of general inspection is to raise the level of operator understanding of the equipment and its maintenance requirements. By operators' participation in development of general inspection, valuable equipment knowledge is gained for future use in diagnosing equipment abnormalities.

This method of developing procedures for inspection is consistent with the TPM objective of empowering small groups to address equipment management issues. Although small groups are empowered to determine what procedures are performed, they must act within the confines of the plant's policies or regulations. Their actions also are shaped by the plant's overall strategy, thus ensuring commonality of data and formats. Commitment and ownership over the process are heightened by the fact that the workers are the primary decision makers as to whether specific activities are best performed by operators or maintenance personnel.

## Autonomous Inspection

Autonomous inspection is the actual transfer of responsibility for equipment inspection. For this to become a reality, two specific activities must be accomplished. First, the previously developed lubrication, cleaning, and general inspection standards must be institutionalized into a system. Second, production operators must be trained in that system and in the technical aspects of the inspections.

Most plants have a Computerized Maintenance Management System (CMMS) that tracks work orders, equipment histories, and preventive/predictive maintenance schedules. These systems usually can be integrated with other support systems such as inventory control, purchasing, accounting, and manufacturing systems. Although most CMMSs were not designed with the production operator in mind, with minor adaptations, they can be used as the backbone of an autonomous maintenance system. Plants lacking a CMMS can develop a manual system for autonomous maintenance, although additional clerical support will be required.

The following are guidelines for integrating your inspection standards into a maintenance system:

- Develop checklists for each operator position and organize them by performance interval. In other words, develop a list for all daily activities, another for all weekly activities, and another for monthly checks. The checklists should be distributed in a logical manner to operators on the different shifts, so that the workload is balanced and takes into account different-shift operating conditions. The check sheets should make extensive use of pictorials to illustrate the tasks to be performed. The illustrations may be an actual part of the check sheet or simply attached to it. Some companies coat the check sheets in plastic and either attach them to the machine or place them in close proximity. They serve a function similar to that of the pre-flight check sheet used by airline pilots before takeoffs. Even though the checks are routine and ingrained in the pilots' memories, their use assures safety and operational requirements. The production operator should use his or her check sheet as religiously as the airline pilot, and complete each check in its proper sequence in much the same manner.

- The maintenance management system should be used to schedule checks that occur at intervals of one week or greater. This provides an electronic record of the check and its performance. Individual inspections become a part of the master preventive maintenance task lists for individual pieces of equipment. Enter the checks in the system as a preventive maintenance task with the production operator assigned as the responsible craftsperson. Since most maintenance management systems do not allow graphic representations of tasks, it is advisable to develop separate representations of the equipment and tasks to be performed. These can be referenced on the computer-generated task lists or schedule.

On-the-job training (OJT), supported by single-point lessons, can be used to train production operators in new inspections, and in the use of the computerized maintenance system to document their completion. Development and administration of the training program is an excellent task for the small groups. Many tasks are generic in nature, however, and should not be "re-developed" by different groups. Simple plantwide activities, such as how to use a grease gun or how to properly torque a bolt, should use common training materials for the whole plant or even company.

Equipment-specific tasks, such as setup adjustments on a machine, should be developed and used only by the small group responsible for that particular area.

By performing inspections, the production operator takes on greater responsibility for the operation of his equipment. He or she is in an excellent position to correlate inspection data with the performance of the machine, thereby opening up new opportunities for improving operating procedures and maintenance practices.

Precedents already exist in North American industry of operators performing autonomous inspections. An example can be seen in the oil industry on many of the offshore platforms in the Gulf of Mexico. Many of these platforms are small and manned by 10 to 20 workers, who function as both the operators and maintenance mechanics for all of the equipment. Although individual workers have special skills, they work as a team for the overall good of the equipment and machinery. For example, a turbine operator/mechanic is totally responsible for the gas turbines on the platform. This includes:

- operation of the turbine
- operating checks
- preventive maintenance procedures
- startup and shutdown activities
- adjustments and calibration of the controls
- decisions on what is required to keep the equipment in top running condition

If an overhaul or changeout of the turbine is required, the turbine operator/mechanic works as part of a team to complete the job. He or she also assists on other areas of the platform, performing both equipment operation and maintenance tasks. The turbine operator/mechanics' use of diverse skills to support optimal equipment performance makes them an advanced example of autonomous maintenance.

In many if not most environments, operator tasks in autonomous maintenance consist principally of inspection and minor adjustments. The ultimate goal of autonomous maintenance in such environments is not to eliminate the maintenance mechanics, but to involve operators in optimizing control.

## Process Discipline

Process discipline is defined as the establishment or improvement of methods and procedures that enable efficiency and repeatability. This broad definition includes such objectives as:

- reducing setup times
- decreasing manufacturing cycle times
- standardizing procedures for handling raw materials
- reducing work-in-progress
- instituting visual control and inspection methods

The goal of process discipline is to reduce variations in the manufacturing process so that consistency, efficiency, and quality are improved.

In typical North American plants, production methods and procedures often vary among the different operating shifts. When replacement operators come on at the start of a shift, they change temperatures, pressures, or running speeds, even though their objective is the same as the previous shift. Although each shift may, in fact, produce product that is entirely within specification, it is accomplished using different methods and controlling parameters. One shift may consistently produce a part that is near upper control limits, while the next shift may produce a part that is consistently near lower control limits. Each shift has a different idea on the best way to produce a part, and each is valid in that the result is on-spec product generated at roughly the same efficiency levels. However, the distinct approaches are not in the best interests of the company. First, there is the issue of the time required to establish and stabilize the different operating options. This is wasted or lost time as it does not add value to the operation. Second, varying operating parameters may affect downstream operations. For instance, varying setup options on one machine may require that changes also be made in the setup options of the next machine. Additionally, frequent changing of setup options on a machine may stress adjustment mechanisms. In effect, unnecessary variations are being implanted in the production process, in contrast to process discipline's goal of reducing variability.

The institutionalization of process discipline, like other levels of autonomous maintenance, is a small group activity. It involves the detailed examination and documentation of the procedures and methods used by the group to collectively contribute to the manufacturing process. Again, documentation is best achieved by graphically illustrating procedures using pictorials or videotapes. As part of process discipline, the following procedures or work methods should be examined:

- manufacturing setup procedures
- shutdown procedures
- startup procedures
- material handling procedures (raw materials and work-in-process materials)
- defective product handling
- workplace layout and organization
- tool, die, and jig layout and organization
- data gathering and reporting procedures

Each of these procedures should be examined by small work groups in their meetings in an effort to standardize the procedures and eliminate waste in effort, time, and materials. The process for examining, improving, and standardizing the procedures includes the following steps:

- List potential work processes that are perceived to be less than optimal in terms of effort or resource.
- Map the present method of performing work in terms of activities, decisions, and interactions with equipment, people, and other systems. See Figure 11 as an example of a typical work flow diagram.
- Examine the work flow diagram in an effort to eliminate multiple ways of accomplishing the same task. Develop the

most effective procedure by eliminating non-value-added steps and reducing time and resource requirements.

- Modify current, documented, work flow diagrams to reflect upgraded methods of performing the work.
- Verify that the upgraded method is superior to historical methods by testing it on the plant floor. Refine the method as required to make it fully functional.
- Train all appropriate workers in the new method. Rather than emphasizing only how to perform individual work steps, focus on the reason for changing and the benefits of standardization.
- Repeat the entire process as required until all work procedures in the plant have been evaluated.

Figure 11 shows how a simple process, such as starting a car, can be mapped.

The diagram provides an effective method of searching for ways to simplify the process. The first step is to identify whether decision points can be eliminated. In the above example, decision points could be eliminated if all cars were automatics rather than some automatics and some manual transmissions. Operation of the cars also would be easier if all of them were fuel injected, thereby eliminating the need to "set" the choke in a cold engine by depressing the accelerator. This type of thought process is typical of what small groups must employ in examining their work processes. The diagrams they develop will be more complex, but the results can be dramatic.

Many plants have made major changes in their procedures as a result of such analyses. One plant discovered it had eight different methods of requesting maintenance work. By standardizing on one common work order system, they had their first accurate look at the size of their backlog. This led to additional changes, eventually enabling them to reduce the average work order cycle time (initiation to completion) from twelve weeks to three days. Another plant had been using fifty types of limit switches supplied by twelve different manufacturers. Through small group activities, they were able to reduce the number of limit switches required to

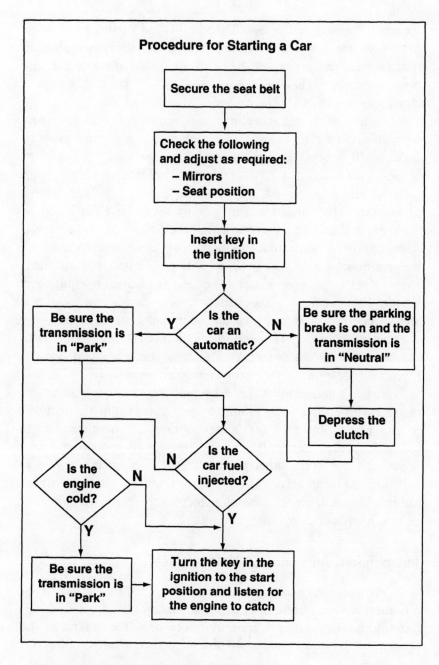

Figure 11. Typical Work Flow Diagram

six from two manufacturers. The elimination of these line items from inventory, and the reduced purchasing efforts, resulted in recurring annual savings of $210 thousand as calculated by the plant controller. The total time expended on the improvement effort was less than 100 labor-hours.

Reduction in changeover time is a major opportunity for many companies. In a glass manufacturing plant, an objective was set to make a 50 percent reduction in the twelve hours required to change over from one type of glass to another. A small group attacked the problem by mapping and examining their current procedures. They discovered that many setup activities could be accomplished prior to shutting down the process for changeover. Although this new approach reduced changeover time to less than the six-hour goal, the problem-solving activities continued. Eventually the team recommended extensive changes to equipment layout. Management authorized necessary capital expenditures, and special jigs were designed and manufactured to simplify the changeover process. The end result was that setup time was reduced to less than twenty-five minutes, and the plant became much more responsive to customer requirements.

Process discipline takes TPM beyond the realm of equipment management and addresses improvement potential in all functions of the plant. Rather than being confined to maintenance, it includes business issues dealing with production procedures and with interfaces to the other plant systems. The concept of zero is expanded to mean zero waste in business and in production procedures. As such, process discipline focuses the entire organization on continuous and rapid improvement.

## Independent Autonomous Maintenance

Independent autonomous maintenance is the point at which the autonomous maintenance process becomes self-sustaining. External forces no longer are required to drive the pursuit of the concept of zero. Empowered small groups are capable of interpreting company goals and policies and of "self-managing" their con-tinuous improvement activities. Minimal outside assistance and management direction is necessary. This state of being is the natural progression of the autonomous maintenance process.

# 6

# Unions and TPM

The basic goals of North American unions do not conflict with the principles of TPM. If union leadership and membership understand TPM, they will not fear it. Management must take responsibility early in the process for involving union leadership to avoid misunderstandings and to clear the way for successful implementation.

Many companies question whether TPM implementation is possible in a union plant. They fear that the unions will object strongly to the shifting of maintenance responsibilities from craftspeople to the production operators. If management's intent behind the shifting of these responsibilities is to reduce head count, unions certainly will resist. But TPM is an improvement methodology focusing on improving equipment management, not reducing personnel. If the objectives and benefits of the improvement process are explained and implemented correctly, employees will throw their full support behind them.

Full TPM implementation is possible in union plants. The degree of acceptance of TPM by plant floor workers is not a function of whether the plant is a unionized or an open shop. Union management and members recognize that in order to compete in today's world marketplace, quality products must be produced as efficiently as possible. By educating employees in how TPM can help the company achieve that objective, management can change people's attitudes and open their minds to new possibilities.

It is helpful to examine the purpose of modern bargaining units in North American plants. Trade unions were formed to provide the hourly work force with a common voice against unfair labor practices, and their power was derived from the solidarity of the workers. Their mission was to improve the quality of work life as measured by compensation, health and safety issues, job security, and general working conditions. Unions also provided a service to the companies by providing a mechanism for training and ensuring consistent job skills of their members.

Employee quality of work life and safety was once the primary issue rallying union members, but companies came to realize that good work environments and safety are not only correct morally, but also make good, solid economic sense. Government agencies have set increasingly stringent requirements and standards for ensuring good working conditions and safe operating practices for all jobs, and there is little doubt that sites are vastly safer today than fifty years ago. Although working conditions and safety are still overriding issues of the unions, their primary focus has changed.

Compensation remains the major focus of unions today. Leadership is often judged in light of gains earned at the bargaining table. Compensation includes salary and associated benefits of:

- health, life, and disability insurance
- educational reimbursement
- vacations, holidays, sick days and other paid time off
- pensions
- cost-of-living (COLA) adjustments

Over the decades, the unions have been extremely successful in achieving significant increases in their total compensation package, and their members' standard of living has risen accordingly.

In recent years, much has been publicized about a decline in blue-collar union membership, which has been accompanied by a reduction in the total number of highly skilled manufacturing jobs. People have voiced concerns that perhaps the unions were too successful in negotiating compensation packages, and had left their companies or plants unable to compete with lower-cost operations. Companies have shut down many older plants, most of which were unionized; and many of the new plants being opened are situated in the South where wage scales are not so high and unions are less prevalent. Offshore manufacturing also has proved alluring to companies, and more and more plant operations are being transplanted to Third World countries. This combination of events has led unions to reexamine their compensation position. They have shown an increased willingness to tie compensation levels to the financial performance of the plant, to trade compensation gains for job security and pension guarantees, or to consider two-tier wage systems.

Although the services sector is growing, the North American manufacturing base is shrinking. The trend appears inexorable. North American jobs continue to face stiff competition from developing third-world countries, particularly in the Far East, while the increasing quality of goods and products has enabled consumers to stretch replacement intervals, effectively adding to a glut in manufacturing capacity. For example, the average life span of a car has increased over the last decade, effectively limiting the demand for new cars. With reduced demand and improved manufacturing techniques, automotive companies and their suppliers are closing underutilized or obsolete plants. The situation has been exacerbated by trade policies that have allowed foreign competitors to capture domestic market share without allowing North American manufacturers equal access to their markets. The result is a shrinking manufacturing base and fewer North American manufacturing jobs.

The decline in manufacturing jobs has made job security the most important issue for unions. Daily headlines trumpet job cutbacks numbering in the thousands, and the trend does not appear to be slowing. Many of the jobs that are available or are being created are low-skill, low-paying, service sector jobs, as opposed to more remunerative high skill jobs.

Recognizing the importance of the job security issue, business leaders and North American unions leaders are striving to build new working relationships that protect the best interests of all parties. New "operating agreements" are being hammered out at bargaining tables across the country, as management and union representatives try to improve companies' competitiveness and worker flexibility in return for secure employment. This trend dovetails with TPM, as increased worker flexibility is applied through autonomous maintenance and multi-skill development of the work force.

## What Can TPM Do for the Unions?

Many companies choosing the TPM path are among the world's most stable organizations, and are leaders in market share, financial stability, and quality of work life. Companies such as Toyota, DuPont, Ford, Texas Instruments, and Motorola are at the forefront of their industries and have been able to sustain stability in fluctuating economies. This stability in uncertain economic times has a direct effect on job security, and is linked to effective communication between management and plant floor workers, including union leadership.

If management initiates TPM activities anticipating head count reductions as the major benefit, the process will fail. If management uses TPM to increase equipment efficiencies, however, the likelihood of union commitment is heightened because employees may see opportunities for greater job security. Concern for job security is not unique to hourly employees. The livelihoods of plant staff, management, and supervisors are also at risk in today's competitive environment. Job security was once governed by an individual's ability to provide value to their organization. Now it depends more on the performance of groups and their success in providing value to the shareholders and company as a whole.

Entire divisions are sold, shut down, or downsized based upon economic results, and union members and management find themselves in the same boat. If unions recognize TPM's capability to positively affect plant economics without reducing head count, they will join wholeheartedly in the improvement process.

## What Can the Unions Do for TPM?

Union endorsement can help guarantee the success of TPM. Normally the improvement process is introduced to plant personnel by management. Unless a constructive relationship already exists between management and union leadership, however, acceptance of the improvement philosophy will not be automatic. TPM education must be offered, so that union officers feel they know enough about the process to recommend it enthusiastically to the rank and file. This active support of union leadership is possible with patience and nurturing.

North American managers worry about opening discussions with the union regarding TPM, especially during the early preparatory stage. Their discomfort lies in discussing an improvement methodology for which specific objectives and methodologies have yet to be defined. Rather than risk involving the union in these early decision points, management mandates the improvement philosophy, and workers are expected to buy in to the program. In this scenario, management retains control over all strategy development, allowing employees to participate only in tactical decisions. To achieve full success in North America, companies must begin to allow unions and workers access to strategic decision-making processes.

If important TPM decisions are made prior to soliciting union involvement, their support will be lukewarm. Although they may offer verbal support of the process, active, on-the-floor activities will be minimal. Employees must be involved and empowered early in the process. Too often they are excluded from early, basic planning stages for fear that they will throw up roadblocks.

*It is never too early to involve union management in the TPM process.* Buy-in may not be immediate, but it is better to solicit their input early in the process and determine where they stand. Sooner or later the two groups must build a level of trust if activities are to succeed. The sooner that process is begun, the sooner both parties can focus on productive activities. Even though strategic decisions will be influenced more greatly by management than by the unions, companies must not forget that implementation works from the bottom up.

## How to Get Union Involvement in the Process

The first key to union involvement is building trust and understanding through effective, honest communication. Step one of the process is to hold regular meetings with union leadership and explain the potential benefits of TPM for the company and employees. Rather than seeking an immediate endorsement, the objective is only to increase their awareness of the philosophy and open their minds to improvement potential in the plant.

The second key to union involvement is comprehensive education. The more unions know about TPM, the less fear they will have. Union leadership should be invited to introductory TPM training sessions and to participate in visits to plants implementing the process. Receptive union officers can offer valuable advice on how to roll out TPM training for their membership, and should be considered as candidates for a "train the trainer" approach.

The third key to union involvement is active participation in the development of the overall TPM plan, starting with union representation on the deployment committee. Employees must play a prominent role in developing the vision, mission, goals, and strategy that will drive TPM. Union leadership sign-off on those activities sends a strong message to the workforce that the union is not in conflict with management on TPM methodologies, but that they see it as a foundation on which they can build.

# 7

# Measuring Overall Equipment Effectiveness

The primary measure of performance in TPM is overall equipment effectiveness (OEE). A powerful component of the TPM process, OEE clearly indicates implementation progress and equipment performance. OEE measures the effective utilization of capital assets by expressing the impact of equipment related losses. Seven types of equipment loss are tracked:

- downtime due to machine breakdown
- time required for setup and adjustments
- time or cycles lost to inefficient startup
- time or cycles lost to tooling
- time or cycles lost to minor stoppages
- operating at less than ideal speed
- producing defective or off-spec product that is rejected, requires rework or repair, or is sold at a lower price

The OEE measure accounts for losses by tracking three critical elements—availability, performance efficiency, and quality rate.

Availability includes machine breakdown or downtime and setup/adjustment losses. Performance efficiency tracks minor stoppages and speed losses, and quality rate tracks product defects and rework. The three components are intended to track all conceivable equipment losses. OEE is calculated as the product of availability, performance efficiency, and quality rate.

$$\text{OEE} = \text{Availability} \times \text{Performance efficiency} \times \text{Quality rate}$$

Detailed definitions of the components of OEE follow.

## Availability

*Availability* is sometimes referred to as *uptime* or *machine utilization*. It is defined as the ratio between operating time and net available time.

$$\text{Availability} = \text{Operating time} \div \text{Net available time}$$

*Operating time* is the time that the equipment actually operates or is actually *loaded*.

*Net available time* is the time that the machine is actually planned to operate or scheduled to operate. For example, in an eight-hour shift, a machine usually is scheduled to operate for eight hours minus any planned breaks or lunch. Other activities also may affect the net available time, such as planned preventive maintenance or time allotted for small group meetings.

$$\text{Net available time} = \text{Total available time} - \text{Planned downtime}$$

*Total available time* is the time that the equipment could run during a shift or other time interval assuming that there is no downtime, either planned or unplanned. For example, the total available time for an eight-hour shift is eight hours.

*Planned downtime* is the time that the equipment is shut down for planned activities. These may include lunch, breaks, meetings, training, small group activities, single-point lessons, and preventive maintenance activities.

Planned downtime = Breaks + Lunch + Planned meetings +
Preventive maintenance

*Unplanned downtime* is the time that the equipment is down due to unplanned events such as breakdowns, setups, adjustments, and other documented stoppages.

Although the above definitions are generally accepted by followers of TPM, disagreements exist as to whether preventive maintenance activities should count as planned or unplanned downtime. The argument for including preventive maintenance activities as unplanned downtime is that many of those activities can be optimized further. For instance, some companies perform excessive or unnecessary preventive maintenance, thereby extending the downtime of the equipment. Optimizing preventive maintenance frequencies and content minimizes downtime, without jeopardizing the health or long-term performance of the equipment. The inclusion of preventive maintenance activities as unplanned downtime (or at least in a category that is tracked as part of the OEE calculation) identifies potential gains in availability. For example, consider the hypothetical practice of changing oil on a machine daily. The procedure is a regularly scheduled preventive maintenance task requiring one hour. Total available time for work during the shift is 8 hours. If preventive maintenance activities are considered planned downtime, the net available time is 7 hours. If one hour of unplanned downtime occurs, the availability would be calculated as:

(7 hours net available time −1 hour unplanned downtime) ÷ 7 = 86%.

If preventive maintenance activities are not considered planned downtime, there would be two hours of unplanned downtime. The new equipment availability would be calculated as:

(8 hours net available time − 2 hours unplanned downtime) ÷ 8 = 75%

The latter calculation reveals a greater opportunity to improve availability and its impact on OEE. Detailed analysis of the situation might expose an opportunity to optimize the preventive maintenance on that equipment item. Perhaps the oil change, with proper planning, could be performed in 30 minutes rather than an hour. Or instead of changing the oil each shift, maybe the oil could be sampled and checked against required specifications. Using this method, the change interval could be extended to once every three days.

The argument for considering preventive maintenance activities as planned downtime is that such activities are vital to the long-term health of the equipment. If preventive maintenance activities are counted as unplanned downtime, short-term availability gains could be made by omitting or skipping the activities. Some supervisors may be tempted to skip the oil change to maximize short-term OEE. Total downtime would decrease one hour and availability would rise to $(8-1) \div 8 = 88.5\%$. The supervisor may be closer to earning his bonus, but his machine may be closer to catastrophic failure.

The decision on whether to include preventive maintenance as planned or unplanned downtime should be made early in the TPM process, and it should be adhered to consistently. The majority of plants and facilities in North America will probably opt to include preventive maintenance as a part of planned downtime. The threat of employees "skipping" preventive maintenance activities will outweigh any gains they perceive possible from the chance to optimize preventive maintenance practices. The more advanced companies, though, will consider preventive maintenance as part of unplanned downtime. Their people will recognize the fallacy of omitting preventive maintenance for short-term gains and will pursue means of shortening or eliminating the need for the practice as part of their autonomous maintenance activities.

## Performance Efficiency

Performance efficiency is sometimes referred to as *throughput efficiency* or *equipment performance efficiency*. It reflects whether equipment is running at its full capacity or speed for individual products. Performance efficiency is defined as the product of ideal cycle time times total parts run divided by the operating time.

$$\text{Performance efficiency} = \frac{\text{Ideal cycle time} \times \text{Total parts run}}{\text{Operating time}}$$

The above formula is a simplification of the formula recommended by JIPM, but provides the same answer. The JIPM formula for calculating performance efficiency is:

Performance efficiency = Overall speed ratio × Net operating rate

The JIPM formula is equally valid but is more difficult to use. The JIPM formula implies that overall speed ratio (the ratio of actual operating speed divided by ideal operating speed) is a number that does not vary. In practice, this ratio may vary over time as operating conditions change. The first formula automatically calculates the average for that time period.

Performance efficiency measures speed losses and losses associated with idling equipment or minor undocumented stoppages. By definition, performance efficiency can never exceed 100 percent. Additional definition of the factors affecting performance efficiency is required.

*Ideal cycle time* defines the ideal production rate of the machine or equipment and is sometimes referred to as the *design speed*. Ideal cycle time (in most cases) is the designed cycle time of the equipment. It reflects the original design of the equipment as defined by purchasing specifications or the manufacturer's data sheets. This may not always be the best way to define the term. Ideal cycle time should be determined on a case-by-case basis. In some instances, operating speeds may have been lowered to eliminate quality problems. Design changes, equipment modifications, or process changes may have altered the original intended operating mode. In establishing ideal cycle times, companies may consider, in addition to the design speed, optimal conditions ( these may vary depending on the product being produced or on changes of equipment in the process), best cycle time ever achieved, or an estimate based on experiences with similar equipment.

A concern at some companies is how to account for ideal cycle time on a piece of equipment that manufactures several products at varying rates. For example, consider the cycle times of a wood cutting machine. The machine is designed to cut different types of wood, with more time required to cut a harder wood such as oak than an equivalent length of pine. How is this accounted for in determining ideal cycle time? Also the difference in product mix may require cuts of varying depths in the wood, which impacts the total time required for the cutting process. How can the varying end product and raw material combinations be accounted for in determining the ideal cycle time?

Determining the ideal cycle time is perhaps the most challenging aspect of developing the OEE. A number of questions have to be answered. Should an ideal cycle time be determined for each product and wood combination, or can an average be developed to include the potential combinations? Does the mix of various woods and various end products vary by shift, month, or season? Although no easy answer may exist for these questions, the following set of guidelines should help in determining ideal cycle times:

- If practical, determine separate ideal cycle times for each potential product and raw material combination. Although this complicates data gathering and reporting, it is the cleanest method to achieve an accurate OEE. This method is impractical if a large number of combinations are possible, or if the combinations change frequently. If possible, try to calculate separate performance efficiency measures and OEE figures based on primary mixes for groups of end products and raw materials.

- If individual performance efficiency calculations are impractical, calculate an average performance efficiency for the machine by using a weighted average of the ideal cycle time over the time period being calculated. For example if oak is cut for six hours and pine for three hours, the ideal cycle time for the period would be a weighted average with oak's ideal cycle time having a weight that is twice that of pine. For example, if the cutting machine ideal cycle time is 30 seconds for oak and 20 seconds for pine, the weighted average ideal cycle time would be:

$$\frac{(6 \text{ hours oak} \times 30 \text{ seconds}) + (3 \text{ hours pine} \times 20 \text{ seconds})}{9 \text{ hours}} = 26.67 \text{ seconds}$$

- This calculation can be difficult in that the new ideal cycle time may need to be figured each day as the number of hours cutting each wood type varies.
- An easier method of calculating performance is to calculate or estimate an overall average ideal cycle time for the typical product mix being produced by the machine. For example, in a typical month, some percentage of product is two-inch oak, another percentage is four-inch pine, and so on. The daily percentages of the product mix may vary enormously, but the monthly or quarterly averages are probably fairly consistent. In determining the average ideal cycle time, one must pick an interval long enough to encompass a normal production cycle. Typically, this time interval is a week or a month. Calculate a weighted average ideal cycle time for a typical week or month of product from a single machine. Use the same time interval when correlating and analyzing the resulting OEE and performance efficiency measures. Analyzing the measures on intervals less than the normal production cycle will tend to show varying results depending on the particular product being produced in that time interval.

Ideal cycle time often is difficult to determine even in situations where the individual machine was purchased for a specific purpose and production rate. For instance, a food processor encountered problems in defining an ideal cycle time for a packaging machine.

The packager was purchased based upon an "Engineered Standard" that was supplied by the manufacturer. Although the engineered standard for the packager was 1200 cases per hour, the best production rate ever achieved at the plant was 900 cases per hour. In this situation the plant and equipment manufacturer were actually using production rates rather than cycle time as the ideal measure. (Cycle times are expressed as time per piece whereas production rates are expressed as pieces per time.) Plant personnel approached the manufacturer for clarification of the standard and asked if any of the equipment manufacturer's customers had actually reached the published specification of 1200 cases per hour. The food processor was put in contact with another plant that used the same machine. This plant was able to make 1200 cases per hour, although not on a consistent basis. Still, this opened people's minds to the real capability and potential of the packager. Since then, the food processor has been able to average a production rate of 1000 cases per hour, and they are striving for the potential 1200 cases per hour.

*Total parts run* is the total number of parts produced during a given operating time, regardless of quality. This number is usually taken from production figures for a set time period or from a meter reading. The major potential for confusion arises when a part is run twice or a product is reblended. This rework occurs because the part or product did not meet specification during the first pass and had to be rerun. In these cases, one part actually gets counted twice.

An example can be seen in the bottling operation of a food packager, in which a quality control check is established downstream of the bottle filler. If the bottle is not filled to a specified level, or the label is not positioned correctly, the bottle is set aside to be refilled or relabeled at a later time. Actual production numbers for the line are not taken as the bottles pass through the bottler, but are tracked downstream of the quality control check. A spot check revealed that almost 5 percent of the bottles going through the filler need to be recycled. By tracking production downstream of the quality control check, the filler rate was being understated by 5 percent. If performance efficiency for the bottler is to be accurately tracked, an accounting must be made for the reworked or recycled bottles.

*Operating time* is calculated in a manner similar to that of availability. Again it reflects the time that the machine is actually loaded and performing work.

If the JIPM formula is used to calculate performance efficiency, the following detailed descriptions will aid in development of the indicator.

*Speed ratio* is the ratio of ideal cycle time to the actual cycle time.

$$\text{Speed ratio} = \text{Ideal cycle time} \div \text{Actual cycle time}$$

If machine speed is calculated using actual parts produced during the operating time (ideal cycle time × total parts run / operating time), speed ratio is equal to the performance efficiency. The speed ratio should never exceed 100 percent.

*Net operating rate* is a measure of the stability of equipment over a set period of time. It directly measures the percentage of time that the machine is not performing useful work due to undocumented minor stoppages or idling.

$$\text{Net operating rate} = \text{Total parts run} \times \text{Actual cycle time} \div \text{Operating time}$$

In calculating net operating rates, some question whether minor stoppages should be accounted for in availability figures or performance efficiency. Some companies charge the stoppage against availability if it is related to equipment malfunction, while material defects, operator errors, or other process upsets are allocated to performance efficiency. This type of allocation may cause confusion. Is a stoppage for a minor adjustment an equipment malfunction, or is it due to variances in raw material? If this distinction is not made, proper countermeasures cannot be implemented to meet the two different problems.

The following guidelines may help in distinguishing between minor stoppages and breakdowns. If the stoppage is documented, no matter what the cause, it should be accounted for in the availability measure. If undocumented due to time shortages or inadequate record keeping, the stoppage should be accounted for in the performance efficiency. This usually means that, as the TPM process matures and record keeping improves, the performance efficiency measure will improve at the expense of the availability measure. As more and more stoppages are documented as to cause and time duration, attention can be focused on the most frequent and costly problems.

## Quality Rate

*Quality rate*, sometimes referred to as *throughput efficiency* or *first run capability*, is defined as the ratio of first run good parts.

Quality rate = (Total parts run − Total defects) ÷ Total parts run

*Total parts run* is the total number of parts produced, whether of good or poor quality, during a given operating time. Total parts run is the same for calculating both performance efficiency and quality rate.

Total parts run = Good parts + Rejected parts + Reworked parts

*Total defects* is the total number of rejected, reworked, or scrapped parts produced during a given operating time. Total defects also includes parts rejected at the customer's delivery location or shipped back to the plant from the customer. These situations require record updates and adjustments to initially published quality measures.

Total defects = Rejects + Reworks + Scrap + Shipbacks

As a result of their formal quality efforts, many organizations already have a good understanding of the above terms and advanced methods of measuring the results of their quality improvement process. In today's world quality should be a given, but such is not the case. Situations still exist in which production, not quality, is the primary focus of operations. For example, a tour through one plant revealed idle workers reading newspapers. When queried about these work practices, management responded that the union contract established set production goals for worker positions. Once these production levels were attained, workers had to remain at their locations, but no longer had to produce additional parts. The most disturbing part of this situation was that goals were based on overall production, and the parts produced did not have to be good quality. That company is now addressing this issue.

Companies constantly must improve quality, with a goal of attaining zero defects. One should not consider scrap, defects, reworks, or shipbacks acceptable. If a zero defects operating environment can be attained for just one hour, it can be accomplished over a shift, a week, a month, or a year.

## OEE Calculation for a Single Machine

Calculating OEE for a single machine is relatively straightforward and depends on adequate training, consistent data collection, and agreed upon procedures or sets of rules. The OEE calculation is an excellent activity to be handled as part of the small group activities outlined in step seven of the TPM process. Adherence to the following steps will enhance the quality of the calculations:

- Train small groups in the methods and reasons for tracking the OEE measure. The training classes should consist of a series of single-point lessons that emphasize the importance of tracking the OEE and that tell how it can help improve plant operations.
- Design a form and format for tracking the input data for the measure. Identify the source of the data, along with the person responsible for its collection. Decide on where and how the data is to be reported. Questions such as "Who should record the data?", "What forms are required?", and "Who should perform the calculations and produce the reports?" must be answered.

- Document the data gathering and reporting process. Large-scale, area-based activity boards are a good place to track the weekly results. Locations near the machines and equipment are good places to plot daily numbers. Monthly numbers should be plotted and displayed at a more central location.
- Have the small groups report and discuss results in their meetings. Report each of the components of availability, performance efficiency, and quality rate. Track individual losses, along with what is being done to improve each of them.

## Using the Overall Plant OEE Measurable

Japanese PM Prize winners typically report a single average OEE number for the entire plant. Unfortunately, they rarely report how that number is calculated. Although calculation of a single machine OEE number is straightforward, the compilation of multiple machine OEE numbers into a single plant number is much more complex. Many options are available on how to compile the plantwide OEE. Prior to their discussion a basic review of OEE is in order. The indicator is a powerful tool for the plant to measure progress on the TPM process. Yet because of the different ways of calculating a plant composite OEE number, it is not necessarily effective in comparing performance of two separate plants, especially if they have different processes. Comparison of machine OEEs are more beneficial and can identify underperforming equipment or single out causes of poor equipment utilization.

JIPM promotes the use of OEE as an indicator of plant performance. An 85 percent OEE is usually considered the threshold for achieving the PM Prize, although a 50 percent OEE improvement from a starting point is also grounds for qualification. Many companies, in particular those outside the automotive industry, have difficulty in understanding how an absolute measure of 85 percent relates to their plant.

The 85 percent OEE goal may not make sense for all types of plants. Its applicability is much greater for discrete manufacturers than for process industry plants. An oil refinery that had an OEE level as low as 85 percent would not be in business long (unless they were forced to operate at less than capacity for lack of market for their products). To illustrate this point, consider the example of Daicel Chemical Industries, Ltd., a large Japanese chemical plant and recent PM Prize winner. When they started their TPM process in 1985, their reported OEE level was already at 92 percent. By 1990, it had risen to 99 percent. How can those numbers be compared to those of a discrete manufacturer? The important issue is the trend of the number, not its absolute value. Is the indicator improving? Are workers in the plant aware of the measure and its importance? Is concrete action being taken to improve it?

## Calculating a Line or Process OEE Number

If all machines were perfectly balanced in terms of production rates and capacities, calculation of a line OEE would be simple. If you have such a process, you will be able to skip this section. But perfectly balanced production lines are a rarity. Plants typically do not have a straight line process in which a part travels from one machine to the next in perfect harmony with other machines in the process. Instead machines are connected in series or parallel, complete with side processes. In order to accommodate these complex processes in calculation of OEE for a process or line, it is best to use a direct calculation of the line or process, that is, one that does not involve calculation of individual machine OEE numbers.

In theory OEE treats an entire line or process as a single machine with a set ideal cycle time equal to the cycle time of the constraining machine in the line. For example, if three machines are connected in series with cycle times of three seconds, two seconds, and four seconds, respectively, the cycle time of the process would be equal to the cycle time of the constraining machine. In this case the constraining machine would be the machine with a cycle time of four seconds. The line as a whole could not manufacture product at a rate faster than one per four seconds. In terms of availability, the key to the whole process is maintaining reliability of the constraining machine (unless the two-and three-second machines are at less than 50 and 66 percent of the availability rate of the constricting machine).

Typically there is some surge or buildup of in-process material in the process between machines. If the surge can handle minor stoppages of the machines that do not constrain the process, the overall production rate of the line or process will not be affected. If the surge is not sufficient to handle the stoppages of other machines, the constraining machine will either be starved for materials, or blocked downstream and unable to process additional materials. In all cases, monitoring the availability and performance efficiency on the constraining machine(s) will provide a good picture of the effective use of your total capital assets.

## Accounting for Quality Losses

There are two ways companies account for product defects from a quality perspective. Under one method, quality defects upstream of the constraining machine are not considered serious, since they do not not affect the output of the line or process, unless they starve the constraining machine of material. Quality defects at the constraining machine or further downstream are treated more seriously since they do reduce total production output. Quality gurus advocate recording all quality defects, regardless of whether they occur upstream or downstream of the constraining machine. Although upstream problems may not reduce production, they still will raise costs for materials, labor, and rework activities. The real reason for differentiating between the two types of quality problems is that downstream problems usually are more costly, and should be addressed on a priority basis. Downstream production losses may prevent the company from meeting its customers' demands. Also, the further the product progresses in the manufacturing process, the more money the company has invested in the form of energy, materials, and labor.

So how do you calculate OEE on a line or process using the constraining machine(s) method? The following is a set of steps to follow for each line or process in a plant or facility. These guidelines have been used on processes that have involved as many as 57 machines with multiple side streams and two simultaneous constraining operations. In such situations creativity is necessary to adapt OEE concepts successfully.

1. Carefully map all steps of the manufacturing process. Mark all machines, transfer points, and material handling operations onto some type of graphic format. This is similar to developing process flow sheets for the plant.
2. Where logical, separate the entire production process into subprocesses. Typically, this means segregating groups of machines that constitute a production area, or grouping machines that are closely coupled. For example, an assembly plant may be divided into several subassembly lines and a final assembly operation, especially if the subassemblies are warehoused, sold separately, or sometimes outsourced.
3. Make separate drawings for each of the lines or processes. On the drawings mark the capacities (or ideal cycle times) for each production machine and transfer (material handling) operation. Locate the constraining operation. Take into account the fact that multiple machines may be performing the same operation, or that multiples of the component being manufactured may be required for the final product.
4. Treat the entire operation as a single machine and use the formula for a single machine OEE calculation with modifications as detailed in the succeeding steps.
5. Availability for the process or line is equal to the availability of the constraining machine operation. If there are multiple machines performing the constraining operation, the availability of the line is equal to a weighted average of the machines performing the operation. The weighting of the average is proportional to the capacity of each machine.
6. Performance efficiency for the process or line is equal to the performance efficiency of the constraining machine(s). Again,

if the constraining operation consists of several machines, the performance efficiency of the line or process is equal to a weighted average of the machines performing the operation. Total parts run is equal to the total parts produced as measured at the constraining operation.

7. Quality rate for the process or line is measured as follows: Total parts run is equal to the total parts through the constraining operation. Defects and rejects are only accounted for if they occur at, or downstream of, the constraining operation. If they occur upstream and starve the constraining operation, the loss will show up in the availability of the constraining operation. If the loss does not starve the constraining operation, it will not affect the production capability although it will affect the production per unit cost.

Line or process OEE will give a good indication of the utilization of capital assets. Figure 12 below provides a simple example for calculating a line or process OEE.

Based on the information in Figure 12, the following facts can be determined:

• In the grinding operation, on average, the requirements for a single piece of product can be satisfied in 1.6 seconds. This represents the average production rate of the two grinders that produce two pieces to make a final product piece.

• In the lathe operation, four pieces can be produced every 2.5 seconds. Since two pieces must be produced by the lathe to supply one product piece, two product pieces can be supplied every 2.5 seconds, or one can be supplied every 1.25 seconds.

• The drill operation can supply the needs of the final product at a rate of one every 0.75 seconds.

• The assembly operation can produce one unit every second.

In this process, the grinding process has the highest cycle time and is the constraining operation. As a result, the entire operation can produce no more than one piece every 1.6 seconds, even though most of the machines have the capability of producing at a

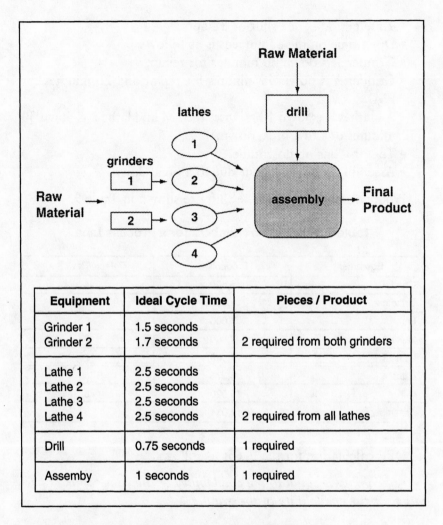

| Equipment | Ideal Cycle Time | Pieces / Product |
|-----------|------------------|------------------|
| Grinder 1<br>Grinder 2 | 1.5 seconds<br>1.7 seconds | 2 required from both grinders |
| Lathe 1<br>Lathe 2<br>Lathe 3<br>Lathe 4 | 2.5 seconds<br>2.5 seconds<br>2.5 seconds<br>2.5 seconds | 2 required from all lathes |
| Drill | 0.75 seconds | 1 required |
| Assemby | 1 seconds | 1 required |

**Figure 12. Example Process Flow Diagram**

much higher rate. This sort of equipment capacity imbalance is quite common to discrete manufacturers of North America.

Availability for the process described above can be expressed as follows:

- Time period is one shift or 8 hours.
- Downtime on the equipment is as follows:
- Grinder 1 is down 30 minutes for repair.
- Grinder 2 is down 45 minutes for repair and 20 minutes for PM.
- All lathes are down 10 minutes for PM and lathe 2 is down 30 minutes due to a breakdown.
- The drill has no downtime.
- Assembly is down 1 hour due to a breakdown.

Production numbers for the shift are shown in Table 9.

**Table 9. Production Numbers for a Process Line**

| Equipment | Production | Defects/Reworks |
|-----------|------------|-----------------|
| Grinder 1 | 15,600 | 44 |
| Grinder 2 | 12,600 | 32 |
| Lathe 1 | 7,000 | 8 |
| Lathe 2 | 7,100 | 6 |
| Lathe 3 | 7,000 | 12 |
| Lathe 4 | 6,974 | 20 |
| Drill | 14,020 | 6 |
| Assembly | 14,014 | 3 |

OEE calculation for the line is as follows.

*Availability is equal to the availability of the constraining operation or the availability of the grinders.*

1. Availability of grinder 1 is:

$$\frac{8 \text{ hour shift} - 0.5 \text{ hours of downtime}}{8 \text{ hours}} = 93.7\%$$

2. Availability of grinder 2 is:

$$\frac{8 \text{ hour shift} - 0.75 \text{ hours down} - 0.33 \text{ hours PM}}{8 \text{ hour shift} - 0.33 \text{ hours PM}} = 90.0\%$$

3. The weighted average for the availability of the grinding operation is:

- Ideal cycle time for grinder 1 is 1.5 seconds or 40 pieces per minute with availability of 93.7%.
- Ideal cycle time for grinder 2 is 1.7 seconds or 35.3 pieces per minute with availability of 90%.
- Weighted average availability is equal to:

$$\frac{(93.7\% \times 40) + (90\% \times 35.3)}{40 + 35.3} = 92.0\%$$

*Performance efficiency calculation for the line is as follows:*

1. Performance efficiency for grinder 1 is :

$$\frac{1.5 \text{ seconds/piece} \times 15{,}600 \text{ pieces}}{7.5 \text{ hours} \times 3600 \text{ seconds/hour}} = 86.7\%$$

2. Performance efficiency for grinder 2 is:

$$\frac{1.7 \text{ seconds/piece} \times 12{,}600 \text{ pieces}}{6.92 \text{ hours} \times 3600 \text{ seconds/hour}} = 86.0\%$$

3. The weighted average (weighted by capacity) for the performance efficiency of the grinding operation is:

$$\frac{(86.7\% \times 40) + (86.0\% \times 35.3)}{40 + 35.3} = 86.4\%$$

*The quality rate for the process is equal to:*

Total parts through the constraining operation (normalized to the final product) − Total defects and reruns at and downstream of the constraining operation ÷ Total parts through the constraining operation.

Total parts through the grinding operation is 28,200 parts divided by 2 parts per assembly, or 14,100.

Total defects and reruns at or downstream of the grinders are as follows:

- Grinder defects are (44 from grinder 1 + 32 from grinder 2) ÷ 2 pieces per assembly, or 38.
- The sum of the lathe defects is 48 pieces ÷ 2 pieces per assembly or 24.
- There are three assembly defects.
- The drill defects are not counted as they do not affect the production capability, unless they are at such a high rate as to starve the assembly operation.

Therefore total defects are 38 + 24 + 3 = 65 defects.

The quality rate for the process is $(14{,}200 - 65) \div 14{,}200 = 99.5\%$.

*The process OEE is equal to availability × performance efficiency × quality rate:*

$$OEE = 92.0\% \times 86.4\% \times 99.5\% = 79.1\%.$$

As stated before, the above example represents a simple process. Many plant processes are not nearly so simple. The key to establishing a meaningful OEE calculation method is the accurate charting of the process with correct ideal cycle times that allow for identification of the constraining or bottleneck operation. The bottleneck operation may change as improvements to the existing process are made. For example, in the above process, improvements to the grinders (or installation of additional, new equipment) may make the grinders so efficient that they can produce at a higher rate. If the rate of production for the grinding operation is improved to more than 96 pieces per minute (the rate of the lathe operation), the lathe operation would then become the constraining operation and the OEE calculation would change.

## Plant OEE Calculation

JIPM uses a "plant OEE" indicator as a TPM measure, but they do not specify a method for its calculation. As a result, winning plants have used several differing methods. If a universal methodology had been applied to all award winning plants, it is likely that some of them would not have attained the necessary 85 percent goal (or 50 percent OEE improvement). A universal standard may not be possible considering the wide variances in manufacturing processes for different industries.

Early winners of the PM Prize were discrete manufacturers who supplied parts to the auto industry. Their plants were relatively small and involved only one or two simple processes. Nippondenso, the first winner of the award, makes small electrical parts. The other Toyota suppliers made items such as plastic bumpers, generators/alternators, transmissions, engine blocks, and stamped body parts. Plant OEEs could be calculated by simply averaging individual machine OEEs. Unfortunately, not all plant processes are that simple, and a more comprehensive method of calculating plant OEE must be devised.

Many plants have used two basic methods for calculating a plant OEE number. They include a process average method and a weighted process average. The first method is a simple numerical average of all of the plant processes that measure OEE. It is easy to calculate and provides a good relative measure of the success of the TPM process in the plant. The second method involves development of a weighted average for all plant processes. The weighting is based upon the value added by each of the processes. Value added can be defined as the value of the product exiting the process, minus the value of the raw or intermediate materials entering the process. This calculation can be complex, but it provides an absolute measure of the process's performance. Since the value added by different plant processes varies, it is important to capture process inequities in the OEE measure through some type of weighting mechanism.

### Calculating a Weighted Process Average

For example, consider a plant that manufactures light bulbs. Three different light bulbs or products are produced at the plant.

## Table 10. Calculating Added Value

| Line | Production Cases | Process OEE | Raw Mat'l Cost | Product Value | Added Value |
|---|---|---|---|---|---|
| A. 100 watt bulbs | 200,000 | 77.8% | $78,125 | $112,500 | $34,375 |
| B. 100 watt bulbs | 225,000 | 65.3% | $87,890 | $126,560 | $39,670 |
| C. 60 watt bulbs | 215,000 | 68.3% | $76,150 | $109,350 | $33,200 |
| D. 60 watt bulbs | 238,000 | 81.4% | $84,960 | $121,050 | $36,090 |
| E. 40 watt bulbs | 143,000 | 42.6% | $59,300 | $64,800 | $5,500 |

The products include 100 watt, 60 watt, and 40 watt models made on five process lines. Two lines manufacture 100 watt bulbs, another two lines make 60 watt bulbs, and one line makes 40 watt bulbs. Production, performance, and value added numbers for the five lines are shown in Table 10.

Notice that the added value for the five lines is simply the difference between the value of the final product and the raw materials.

If one were to use the process average to calculate the plant OEE for the light bulb plant, the calculation would be the simple average of the five process line OEEs or 67.3 percent. The plant would be motivated to improve the OEE on line E, the 40 watt bulb line. Although a 20 point rise in the OEE level of line E would increase the plant OEE level by 4 points, it would not increase the profits of the plant correspondingly, since the added value for that line is relatively small in comparison with the other lines. The advantage of this averaging method is that it is simple to calculate and understand. If there are five plant processes, improvement in one of the processes by five points will affect the plant OEE level by 1 percent.

If the plant used the weighted average method to calculate the overall OEE, the result would be as shown in Table 11.

In the above case the percent of value equals the added value for the line divided by the total of the added value for all lines. The OEE component equals the percent of value added times the line OEE. The total plant OEE is equal to the sum of the OEE compo-

## Table 11. Calculating Weighted Average

| Line | Process OEE | Added Value | Percent of Value | OEE Component |
|------|-------------|-------------|------------------|---------------|
| A. 100 watt bulbs | 77.8% | $34,375 | 23.1% | 18.0% |
| B. 100 watt bulbs | 65.3% | $39,670 | 26.7% | 17.4% |
| C. 60 watt bulbs | 68.3% | $33,200 | 22.3% | 15.2% |
| D. 60 watt bulbs | 81.4% | $36,090 | 24.2% | 19.7% |
| E. 40 watt bulbs | 42.6% | $5,500 | 3.7% | 1.6% |
| Total | | 148,835 | 100% | 71.9% |

nents for all of the lines. In this case the plant OEE equals 71.9 percent, which is significantly different than the 67.3 percent that was calculated by the simple average method. Using the weighted average approach, the focus on OEE improvement for the entire plant would not be on line E. A 20 point increase in line E OEE would raise the plant OEE by only approximately 1 percent, while a 20 point raise in line B's OEE would increase plant OEE by approximately 5 percent. Logically, the plant should place higher priority on improving the OEE level of line B instead of line E. The weighted average method of calculating plant OEE clarifies where attention and resources should be allocated.

The disadvantage in using the weighted average method lies with the difficulty in determining the added value for each line or process in the plant. The added value of the processes will change depending on the latest pricing of the raw materials as well as the actual value of the end products. Such variances can only be tracked by the accounting department or plant controller. If the added value of each plant process is nearly equal, the advantage of using the weighted average method is limited further. When all value added numbers are equal for different processes in the plant, either method of calculating the plant OEE level will yield the same figures. The advantage of using the weighted average method is that it integrates overall equipment performance with the actual financial performance of the plant. Although more effort is required to calculate the plant OEE using the weighted average method, it provides a more useful number. If the weighted average method is used, the plant controller should be able to calculate the net value to the plant resulting from an increase in OEE levels of one, five, or ten points. This number may be dynamic in terms of costs of raw materials or varying end product values, but it still can be viewed as a direct benefit to the plant in terms that satisfy both the financial and production managers.

## Corporate or Division OEE Measures

Some companies attempt to calculate an overall division or corporate OEE number. Generation of these numbers requires a method similar to that of the weighted average methodology. Individual plant OEE numbers can be weighted by the relative value added by each plant. These numbers can be used by corporate management as both economic and equipment performance measures, as well as a means to measure the effective use of the company's capital assets.

## Showing the Results of OEE

Calculating a true, meaningful performance measure is extremely important to any improvement process. Equally important is the visibility and communication of the measure to the people who can impact it. Special emphasis should be placed on the OEE trend. For the equipment, process, or plant to be improving, the OEE slope or trend must be positive. The greater the slope of the OEE trend line, the faster the improvement. Therefore, it is important to show all OEE measures in a graphical format, so that the slope of the line is the first item viewed.

One European plant in the automotive components industry developed an OEE chart for each piece of equipment. All small group activity meetings started with a review of the latest OEE measures which were graphed and posted in each plant area. The plant OEE number also was graphed and shown on prominent walls near the entrance to the plant, on the plant bulletin boards, and on the first page of the monthly plant performance report. In addition to the overall OEE number, calculation of the individual equipment losses (breakdown loss, startup loss, tooling loss, minor stoppages, speed losses, and quality defects) were tracked and displayed. Each loss was attacked separately to find and correct the root cause, resulting in permanent fixes to equipment losses. All plant personnel understood the importance of the measures and took visible pride in how they had improved them by addressing equipment issues.

The OEE should be used as a scorecard for plant performance. Use it to your advantage by performing the following:

1. Calculate, graph, and display the results to all plant personnel.
2. Use small group activity meetings to explain the measure—from how it is calculated to what the financial rewards to the plant are for its improvement.
3. Train plant personnel in OEE calculation methods so they understand the effect of any form of waste.
4. Use activity boards, bulletin boards, space on SPC boards, or any other visible space to post results for all to see and review.

## The Power of OEE

OEE is the most effective measure for driving plant improvement. It continually focuses the plant on the concept of zero waste. When used effectively, its power is awesome. Just the calculation and display of the measure can help drive performance improvement without any other action taken by management. People want to provide value in their job and will focus on what is perceived to be important. We are what we measure. If we measure what is important, our efforts will be rewarded.

# 8

# TPM and
# Theory of Constraints /
# Continuous Flow Manufacturing

One manufacturing strategy receiving major attention recently is continuous flow manufacturing (CFM). This philosophy concentrates on the goal of maximizing throughput while simultaneously reducing inventory and operating expenses. By eliminating lost time in the manufacturing process, CFM expands the concept of zero to include wasted time. Included in the manufacturing strategy is an improvement process entitled Theory of Constraints (TOC) which outlines a methodology to achieve continuous flow manufacturing goals.

Although Theory of Constraints/continuous flow manufacturing and TPM have entirely different roots, the processes support one another. When both are effectively coordinated in implementation they can provide an unbeatable team. Before discussing more extensively how Theory of Constraints/continuous flow manufacturing and TPM complement one another, an explanation of the Theory of Constraints process and continuous flow manufacturing concepts is in order.

## What Is Continuous Flow Manufacturing?

The theory of continuous flow manufacturing was developed by Eliyahu M. Goldratt and was first described in an educational novel entitled *The Goal*,[8] co-authored by Goldratt and Jeff Cox. This entertaining book describes the philosophy and its accompanying methodology (Theory of Constraints) by using the story of a fictitious plant manager as he struggles to make his plant profitable. Goldratt has established a training institute in New Haven, Connecticut (the Avraham Y. Goldratt Institute) and published an additional book, *The Race*,[9] further promoting the strategy as the solution for optimizing manufacturing operations.

Continuous flow manufacturing can best be defined as a manufacturing philosophy which strives to continually reduce manufacturing inefficiencies through improvements in logistics. This can be complementary to TPM's focus on equipment related losses.

CFM is a common sense approach that concentrates on turning raw materials into finished products as quickly as possible and with no wasted effort. Also, the production philosophy is time-based and optimizes the material flow and logistics of the whole organization as opposed to productivity on individual segments of the production process. Continuous flow manufacturing principles promote focus on improving production process bottlenecks or constraining operations to the exclusion of all other improvement efforts. The goal is to increase throughput while simultaneously decreasing inventories and true operating expenses.

Continuous flow manufacturing starts with the basic premise that the goal of any plant organization is to make money now and in the future. An efficient plant that is not profitable does not provide value, and should be examined for potential elimination or sale. Making money is defined in terms of net profit and return

8. Eliyahu Goldratt and Jeff Fox, *The Goal*, Croton-on-Hudson, NY: North River Press, 1984.

9. Eliyahu Goldratt and Jeff Fox, *The Race*, Croton-on-Hudson, NY: North River Press, 1986.

on investment. Definitions of terms which are used in continuous flow manufacturing are as follows:

- *Throughput.* The rate at which any organization generates cash through sales of product, services, or assets. This is equal to sales minus variable expenses.
- *Investment.* Money that an organization spends on things that can ultimately be turned into cash. This includes capital equipment (depreciated) and inventories.
- *Operating expense.* Money spent on converting investments into throughput.
- *Variable expense.* The subset of operating expense that varies with business volume.
- *Net profit.* Profit that is equal to throughput minus operating expense.
- *Return on investment.* The sum that is equal to net profit (or throughput minus operating expense) divided by investment.
- *Productivity.* The amount equal to throughput divided by operating expense.

The goal of the organization is to increase return on investment and net profit. This can be done by any of the following means.

*Decrease operating expense.* If operating expenses are decreased, net profit will increase correspondingly. Since return on investment is directly proportional to net profit, it also will go up if operating expense is decreased. Most organizations try to make improvements in net profit and return on investment by decreasing operating expenses. Although great improvements can be made by concentrating on reducing operating expenses, it is subject to the law of diminishing returns. There is also always the temptation to decrease operating expenses for short-term net profit increases, which only jeopardizes future earnings potential.

*Decrease investment.* If investment is decreased, it will increase return on investment, but it will not affect net profit. Unfortunately for most organizations, the majority of this investment is already expended and there are few things an organization can do to decrease it. Also, in many situations, a tradeoff must be made between investment and operating expense. For example, a more efficient machine (requiring less energy or other resources to run) may be more expensive than a less efficient machine. The organization must make an economic analysis between operating costs and investment. Again, there is the temptation to decrease operating expenses for short-term net profit increases, which jeopardizes future earnings potential.

*Increase throughput.* Improving throughput increases net profits and return on investment simultaneously. In the traditional view of cost control, very little effort is allocated to increasing throughput. Most activities are focused on controlling costs, rather than controlling flow. Throughput can be increased, though, with little or no increase in investment, if appropriate focus is applied. Continuous flow manufacturing concentrates almost entirely on increasing throughput. Increasing throughput only increases profits and returns on investment if there is a market for the new additional product. If the organization as a whole cannot increase sales to accommodate the increased throughput, then increased throughput will provide no additional net profit or return on investment. In this situation, Goldratt would pinpoint the sales organization as a constraining operation. It is important to note that, although it is not mentioned by Goldratt, TPM is an excellent process for increasing throughput.

## What Is the Theory of Constraints?

Continuous flow manufacturing uses an improvement process entitled Theory of Constraints to increase throughput.

Theory of Constraints uses a five-step methodology, as shown in Figure 13.

1. *Identify the manufacturing process constraint*
   What machine or operation in the manufacturing process has the lowest overall production capability? Identification of this constraining operation is key to the entire CFM process. Usually, the major production constraint is the machine with the slowest overall speed. This deficient operation may be obscured by inventory buffers or scheduling practices, but it

must be discovered in order to proceed with the CFM implementation.

*2. Exploit the manufacturing process constraint*
The organization must make every effort to keep the constraint productive at all times. This may mean operating the constraint on additional shifts, staffing the constraint to ensure full production, or moving quality checks upstream of the constraint to ensure that it is always working on quality pieces. Unfortunately, Goldratt suggests few substantive methods for increasing constraint throughput. He delegates to the reader the responsibility for devising methods to optimize operations of the constraint.

*3. Subordinate to the constraint*
All other activities of the organization must be subordinated to the constraint. This means that the plant should operate or schedule other machine operations so that the constraint is

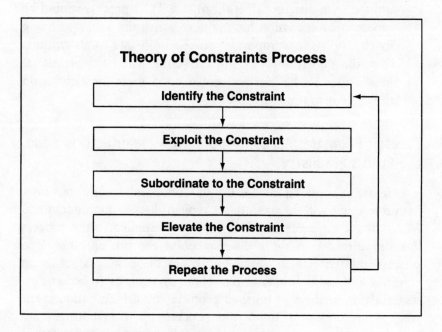

**Figure 13. Theory of Constraints Process**

always loaded or operational. There is no need to work on speeding up other machines in the production process, since the constraint is the limiting factor. All efforts should be concentrated on improving the constraint's performance.

### 4. Elevate the constraint

Make investments in the constraint to improve its capacity and throughput. The ultimate objective is to elevate the capacity of the constraint to a level in which it is no longer the constraining operation. This may involve engineering upgrades, purchasing additional capacity, or converting other machines to augment the constraint. Once again, Goldratt does not suggest specific procedures or methods on how to accomplish this. TPM's step seven, improve the effectiveness of each piece of equipment, would be an excellent method for elevating the constraint.

### 5. Repeat the process

Once the constraining operation is moved (the capacity is limited by a different operation), the TOC process should be repeated by searching for the new constraint and upgrading its capability. It is important to communicate to all workers that the constraint has moved. Otherwise, organizational inertia may lead to further efforts to increase throughput on the old constraining operation.

## Theory of Constraints/Continuous Flow Manufacturing and the Process Industry

Benefits in applying the Theory of Constraints/continuous flow manufacturing will be greatest for typical discrete manufacturers. Many of the concepts of TOC have been applied to the process industry already, so the remaining gains are not as large. The process industry has no choice but to practice concepts similar to continuous flow manufacturing. Their inventories (whether raw materials, in process, or finished product) are difficult and expensive to store. Often times the process plant inventories are unstable, under pressure, at elevated or depressed temperatures, or occupy so much volume that storage of the inventory is impossible. Interruptions in the process industry production process are expensive and difficult, and plant shutdowns and startups are very structured and time consuming. As a result, most process plants are already practicing the philosophy of continuous flow manufacturing. In effect, CFM is designed to encourage the discrete manufacturing plants to operate and react like process plants.

### Measures of Success

One of the beauties of Theory of Constraints/continuous flow manufacturing is that it aligns the manufacturing process with the key economic indicators of net profit and return on investment. These are normally tracked by accounting in most organizations and can be directly correlated as an output measure to Theory of Constraints/continuous flow manufacturing. An additional powerful measure for the improvement process is throughput or throughput efficiency. Throughput efficiency is defined as the percent of maximum throughput that the constraint operation is running. It can be calculated as:

$$\text{Throughput efficiency} = \frac{\text{Actual throughput}}{\text{Maximum potential throughput} \times 100}$$

Goldratt directly states that the most effective improvements in the manufacturing process are made by increasing throughput. In addition to throughput efficiency, throughput per constraint minute can be calculated to highlight the true cost of downtime on the constraint operation. The formula is as follows:

$$\frac{\text{Throughput}}{\text{Constraint minute}} = \frac{(\text{Sales} - \text{Variable expense}) \div \text{Parts run}}{\text{Cycle time}}$$

Furthermore, it is possible to calculate the cost of unplanned downtime as being:

$$\text{Cost of unplanned downtime} = \frac{\text{Unplanned downtime} \times \text{Throughput}}{\text{Constraint minute}}$$

All of these calculations make it possible to directly correlate the constraint throughput performance with financial performance.

Another measure commonly used to evaluate the Theory of Constraints/continuous flow manufacturing process is manufacturing cycle time (MCT). MCT is defined as the elapsed time from when the raw material first enters the production facility until it leaves the facility as shipped finished product. The easiest way to measure MCT is to mark a particular part of raw material with a time/date stamp when the raw material is received at the receiving dock. This time/date stamp is then compared to the actual shipping time and date that the former raw material leaves as part of the finished product. The elapsed time is measured, reported, and trended as a measure of progress in Theory of Constraints. The lower the number, the closer to successful continuous flow manufacturing. Lowering MCT accomplishes two things.

First, lower MCT means lower inventories. Since inventory can be thought of as investment, lower investment will increase return on investment. Lower inventories also mean shorter delivery times or more responsiveness to your customers. Throughput is increased, back orders are worked through the system, in-process inventories (and jobs) are reduced, and as a result production schedules are shortened. In theory, a 50 percent reduction in inventories should equate to a 50 percent decrease in delivery (order to shipment) times. Shorter delivery times provide more satisfied customers, leading to future increased sales. Those additional sales can drive even greater improvements in throughput.

MCT can be lowered effectively by decreasing all inventories (raw materials, in-process, and finished product) and establishing smaller batch sizes. This can be accomplished only if the equipment processing the materials is operating predictably and reliably. A major reason that plants retain in-process inventories is to guard against potential machine breakdown. With sufficient in-process inventories, the effect of a machine breakdown is minimized, because downstream equipment can work off stored inventories while the broken machine is being repaired. Elimination of these inventories increases the probability that the line will be starved for material. Goldratt points out that these stoppages are not as serious if they do not involve the constraining operation. When the constraining operation is involved, process throughput is affected. In order to effectively reduce MCT, the constraining operation must be reliable and have a low probability of breakdown.

## How to Correlate Theory of Constraints with TPM

If TOC/CFM and TPM are examined closely, one can see that the processes are complementary. The goals of each process are virtually the same, although they are expressed in different terms. TPM enables continuous and rapid improvement to gain or maintain a competitive advantage in manufacturing. The goal of Theory of Constraints/continuous flow manufacturing is to make money. A competitive advantage in manufacturing will allow an organization to make money now and in the future.

The major measurement in Theory of Constraints is throughput. Improvements in throughput allow additional sales, additional net profit, and additional return on investment. The major measurement in TPM is overall equipment effectiveness (OEE). Process or line OEE as defined in chapter 7 can be correlated directly with throughput. OEE is actually the percent of potential throughput. It can be expressed as:

$$\text{Process OEE} = \frac{\text{Actual throughput}}{\text{Maximum potential throughput} \times 100}$$

This is exactly the same formula as the one given for throughput efficiency. As such, improvements in throughput can be tracked effectively using the process OEE calculation presented in chapter 7.

Whereas Theory of Constraints does not suggest a method for increasing throughput, TPM does. OEE can be increased by systematically addressing the six major losses of:

- breakdowns
- setups and adjustments
- minor stoppages

- speed (less than ideal)
- rejects
- startup

These six losses can also be substantially reduced in some environments using the seven levels of autonomous maintenance. CFM can be used to prioritize autonomous maintenance activities by focusing efforts on the constraint operation.

As stated previously, low MCTs require high reliability of the constraining operation. TPM provides the tool to increase this reliability.

Theory of Constraints strives to improve throughput of the constraining operation (referred to as "exploiting the constraint"). Step seven improvement activities and step eight, which involves autonomous maintenance, help drive OEE improvements. Autonomous maintenance and focused improvement activity aimed at the constraining operation will more than likely drive improvements in throughput. Step nine of the TPM process, establishment of a planned maintenance system in the maintenance department, will support further improvements in OEE and throughput.

Continuous flow manufacturing and Theory of Constraints are complementary processes. When worked together, they can drive tremendous improvements in any manufacturing organization. Continuous flow manufacturing does an excellent job of prioritizing areas for improvement and aligning the improvement process to the financial goals of net profit and return on investment. TPM provides specific methods of improving the manufacturing processes which have been prioritized by the Theory of Constraints. Throughput efficiency and line or process OEE are virtually the same measurement of performance.

# 9

# TPM and Benchmarking

One philosophy that has gained credence in recent years is benchmarking. Although this approach has been employed primarily at higher levels of management, it offers significant potential benefits to the autonomous groups used in TPM. In his book on the subject,[1] Robert Camp defines benchmarking as "the search for best practices." Fifteen years ago such searches were virtually nonexistent in North America. A smug sense of self-satisfaction and complacency permeated companies because they had long dominated international and national markets. At the plant level, few companies had interest in how competitors managed their manufacturing operations. They tended to guard information on their own manufacturing processes, and evinced little interest in seeking out improved manufacturing and reliability methods. Lessons to be

---

1. Robert C. Camp, *Benchmarking: The Search for Industry Best Practices That Lead to Superior Performance*, Milwalkee: Quality Press/Quality Resources, 1989.

learned from others' systems, organizational structures, and management methodologies were dismissed, falling before the NIH (not invented here) syndrome. Managers, supervisors, and workers considered their plants unique and therefore felt their plant had nothing to gain from another plant's experiences. Rather than understanding that plants are similar and face common problems, organizations claimed that differences set them apart. The age of a plant and its equipment, the educational or age levels of personnel, and the different product mixes were all set forth as reasons why one plant could not copy modified practices from another.

As competitive pressures increased over time, profit margins shrank, market share was lost, and plants shut down. Only then was the urgency of the situation acknowledged. Companies recognized that past business practices no longer sufficed. Changes would have to be dramatic and continuous. As companies grappled with the need to change, they started reaching out to other organizations, including competitors, to learn how they had revived their businesses. An openness to new ideas, thoughts, and methods was encouraged by key people. Out of these beginnings surfaced formal benchmarking practices.

As indicated earlier, benchmarking is "the search for best practices." Although some companies still restrict this search to companies in their own industry, many have taken a broader approach. They want to learn from the people who employ the most creative and innovative practices so they can leapfrog their competition. As a result, you find discrete manufacturers visiting continuous process plants and car manufacturers studying mail order companies, all in an attempt to learn how leading companies manage key business processes.

The rapid growth of TPM in North America in recent years owes much to the emphasis on benchmarking. As management recognized the critical role of maintenance in their operations, they sought out companies that had achieved major gains in improving equipment reliability and controlling maintenance costs. Their searches led them more and more frequently to plants that had implemented TPM or its variations. After studying how TPM was applied, managers attempted to carry the new concepts to their own plants. Their levels of success varied widely.

As companies contemplate the potential gains from TPM implementation, they need to thoroughly investigate the hurdles they will encounter. One of the best ways to do this is by benchmarking the TPM practices and results achieved at other organizations. By studying the experiences of others, companies can avoid common missteps or unnecessarily protracted implementations. Benchmarking activities also provide a method of convincing various levels of the organization, including worker groups, of the value of TPM. Providing people with the opportunity to physically observe TPM in action carries considerably more impact than asking them to commit to a philosophy about which they have only read. Discussion of drawbacks and benefits with peers from other plants is the type of contact employees need to develop passionate commitment.

Many companies conduct one-time visits to other plants simply to help determine whether they should proceed with a similar implementation. In doing so, they miss out on many of the major gains possible from benchmarking. The smartest companies recognize that benchmarking is a continuous process. As such, they are looking to build formal networking relationships with other organizations. By maintaining a long-term relationship with a select number of plants, an organization can draw on a broad base of learning experiences to accelerate its improvement process. If TPM-committed plants link together to share their successes and innovative approaches, the NIH syndrome gradually disintegrates. At some point, though, the networked plants will exhaust the information that can be gained from one another. Prior to that point, they should have sought out new companies with which they can network to reinvigorate their improvement process.

## Finding a Benchmarking Partner

In building formal benchmarking and networking relationships, a key challenge is to find appropriate, willing partners. Many companies still are reluctant to embark on such journeys. Plants in the same industry may fear losing proprietary information to competitors; nonunion companies may not wish to expose their employees to union environments; and some companies simply are philosophically against sharing information.

Still, a concerted search for a benchmarking partner will always be successful. Professional and networking organizations, such as the Society for Maintenance and Reliability Professionals (SMRP) and the American Institute for Total Productive Maintenance (AITPM), provide a variety of benchmarking services to members. Members of these groups typically can indicate whether their corporation or individual plants are receptive to networking. Attending trade shows and maintenance conferences is another way to contact representatives of companies with which an organization might wish to establish a relationship. Consulting firms, drawing on the relationships they have built with clients over numerous years, can help place interested organizations together.

## Choosing the Benchmarking Team

When companies join forces to benchmark with one another, they need to determine who are the best candidates to conduct the visits. The number and type of people chosen varies depending on whether the benchmarking is based on a one-time visit or a long-term relationship. There are certain characteristics and capabilities that should be exhibited by the visiting team. Members should have:

- An intimate understanding of how work is currently performed in their organization, so that they can identify the variances or gaps with how work is performed at the host site.
- An open mind and willingness to consider alternative, innovative approaches to conducting business.
- A positive reputation among their peers, so that plant personnel will be more receptive to information and ideas brought back from benchmarking activities.
- Leadership skills enabling them to guide their peers in developing and implementing new practices or modifications of current procedures.

The benchmarking team should consist of people from multiple levels and functions of the organization. A sample team might consist of the following:

- maintenance or production manager
- maintenance supervisor
- production supervisor
- maintenance craftspeople (1 mechanical and 1 E&I)
- operators (2)
- engineer

Obviously, the size of the visiting team will be determined by how many people the host site will accept. A large group places a greater burden on them, but they usually will be receptive if they can make a similarly sized return visit. A mixture of production and maintenance personnel is critical, as TPM requires both groups to accept accountability and ownership for equipment. New practices will likely require that maintenance-related activities be shared.

## The Benefit of In-Depth Observation

Optimal benchmarking is achieved through the establishment of long-term relationships involving multiple site visits. Few people are capable of absorbing and understanding the subtleties of how an organization functions based on one or two visits. Two process industry plants, one from the Gulf Coast and another from the West Coast, serve as an example of the drawbacks of short-term benchmarking visits. Refineries have used numerous organizations to measure their financial and operating performance and evaluate the effectiveness of their practices. One company, used by many refineries worldwide, organizes the plants into quartiles, with a first quartile ranking indicating superior performance.

In this particular situation, a fourth quartile refinery arranged to make a three-day visit to a first quartile plant. The fourth quartile facility hoped to learn what practices enabled its competitor to achieve its high ranking. After the visit, the guest team expressed disappointment. The low performing plant employees felt they were doing all the same things as the high performer. For instance, they both had area-based maintenance forces, used computerized maintenance management systems, planned and scheduled maintenance repairs, and so forth. They were right! Both plants were employing the same or similar practices. What separated them was the quality and level of sophistication with which the practices were employed.

For example, the quality of maintenance planning and scheduling varied greatly between the two organizations. In one, the meetings were held haphazardly, an excessive number of people were asked to attend, the agenda was unclear, and people arrived unprepared. Duplicate jobs ended up on schedules and uncertainty existed as to what repairs had been completed. The first quartile refinery, on the other hand, held succinct, to-the-point meetings with a minimal number of people who came prepared to discuss the key items. Yes, both organizations did planning and scheduling that were supported by written procedures. Yet the quality with which those activities were executed clearly differentiated the two refineries and was reflected in their ability to complete work in a timely, cost-effective fashion. Unfortunately, the benchmarking visit by the fourth quartile plant did not allow enough time for the participants to recognize or understand the differences in how planning and scheduling, as well as other maintenance practices, were carried out. The result was the erroneous impression that the two refineries did things the same way.

## Cross-Industry Networking Groups

Networked companies frequently will be from different industries. In one situation, three companies joined together from the pulp and paper, chemical, and aluminum industries. Although their products differed, the companies exhibited many similar characteristics. For instance:

- They were all continuous process plants.
- Each facility had been built in the previous ten years.

- Each organization was considered a leader in its industry.
- All three companies were nonunion.
- Each company employed innovative, creative approaches in managing their business such as using self-managing teams or having operators and mechanics periodically alternate positions or responsibilities.

Most networking groups err in not looking closely enough at each other's business processes. They hold meetings and discussions, but never intimately examine why each company is successful. The companies in this example took special care to move beyond superficial analysis. The process around which they constructed their network was as follows:

1. *Meeting frequency.* The groups decided that they needed to meet frequently enough to ensure that previously shared information was not forgotten. Each subsequent meeting could then build on a firm informational database. In this instance, the companies agreed to meet quarterly.
2. *Meeting location.* The first meeting was held at a neutral location, so that representatives of each company had an opportunity to become comfortable with one another in a nonthreatening environment. Subsequent meetings were then rotated. The host company was responsible for coordinating all activities for their assigned meeting. To build rapport between the groups, several nonbusiness activities were also scheduled for each meeting. Tours of local city attractions, social dinners, and other events helped the participants build interpersonal relationships and eased the flow of information as trust was generated.
3. *Participants.* Members of each company's team included managers, supervisors, and worker representatives. Normally each team included five to eight people. Some were permanent members and attended every meeting to promote continuity. Other members attended on a rotating basis depending on the subject of the individual meeting.

4. *Content.* The intent was to give the participants a real-world look at each other's organizations and methods. It was expected that groups would then take what they learned back to their own organizations, make necessary modifications to fit their particular environment and culture, and implement the new concepts or practices. The meetings typically lasted two days. Half of the time was oriented to presentations and discussions. Normally the host company demonstrated what they considered to be their innovative, creative practices. This was followed by question and answer sessions. A particular benefit to the host company is that they were allowed to have as many people as possible from their organization sit in on the session. The other half of the time was allocated to touring the plants and observing operations. For example, some visiting plants would have one of their mechanics or instrument technicians spend a full or half day with the equivalent person from the host organization. This allowed them to see specifically what equipment was used in the plant, how it was maintained, and how work was organized and evaluated.

The experiences gained from this networking were invaluable, and the companies were able to adapt new ideas to their own organizations.

Most intercompany networking falls short of its potential. Too often companies are satisfied with general tours of another site. They hear what they are supposed to hear and see what they are supposed to see. Only intensive time on-site will reveal the subtleties of how a company really goes about its business.

The potential gains from benchmarking and networking must not be overlooked by TPM-committed organizations. As autonomous teams are formed, they should have opportunities to visit other sites as part of their learning process. Naturally, many of the locations visited should be companies practicing or in the process of implementing TPM. Non-TPM companies should not be overlooked, however. Many companies are implementing practices that, although not specifically designated as TPM activities, are complementary to TPM philosophies. The intent of autonomous groups should be to seek out organizations that are applying innovative creative concepts, regardless of the title or heading under which they are masquerading

## Quantitative and Qualitative Benchmarking

There are two critical aspects to benchmarking: quantitative and qualitative. Quantitative benchmarking focuses on evaluating "hard number" performance indicators such as equipment uptime or emergency work levels. This quantitative comparison typically needs to be done within the same industry. The second aspect of benchmarking is qualitative in nature. It involves the regular practices and procedures that are employed such as work planning and scheduling techniques.

Too often, companies focus exclusively on the quantitative aspect of benchmarking. The indicators are easy to understand, appear to be objective evaluators of performance, and can be visually arresting if graphically portrayed. Shortcomings are common, though. The greatest failing is that companies do not compare apples to apples. The definitions for individual indicators vary, or they are composed of information drawn from different sources. For instance, two companies may track an indicator on the number of turns per year for maintenance parts. One company may track all parts in compiling its indicator, including expensive, slow-moving capital spares, while the second company may exclude that category. This difference in calculation certainly skews the results, and could lead to erroneous conclusions as to who has the overall faster-moving inventory. Another failing of the quantitative focus is that compilation of the indicators does not necessarily reveal what can be done to impact them positively or negatively.

The qualitative aspect of benchmarking is as important, if not more so, than the quantitative indicators. If companies correctly employ best practices, those practices automatically will drive improved performance. The gains will show up on the financial and reliability indicators of the organization. Companies often overlook the actual practices because it is more cumbersome and laborious to identify them than it is to simply look at some graphs of performance. Companies also need an intimate understanding of their own procedures, so that they can identify gaps and differences. Too often, this preparation prior to making a benchmarking visit to a host plant is done superficially or not at all. People become excited about the opportunity to travel and neglect the preparatory homework that determines the success of the visit.

To take full advantage of benchmarking opportunities, companies must determine in advance what they will benchmark quantitatively and qualitatively. The following section identifies potential samples of both. The lists are not intended to be all encompassing, but should provide organizations with a robust grouping from which they can choose as well as with stimulation for thinking about the issues.

### Quantitative Indicators

There are literally hundreds of potential quantitative performance indicators. The following are broken into three basic groups. They are:

*Macro-indicators.* These overview indicators are typically most valuable for upper management groups. Although worker groups may understand them, it is difficult to see how they can impact them on a personal basis. Examples are:

- maintenance expense dollars as a percent of replacement asset value (RAV)
- maintenance expense dollars per unit produced
- maintenance expense dollars as a percent of plant controllable expenses
- regulatory compliance indicators

*Micro-indicators.* These indicators are normally more meaningful to work groups and lower levels of supervision, because these groups are accustomed to working with such measures in some capacity and often understand how they can be impacted. The micro-indicators may reflect financial or equipment performance. Examples are:

- budget compliance (budget versus expense)
- monthly expense dollars per type of equipment (pumps, motors, etc.)
- percent overtime
- percent emergency work
- number of call-ins
- equipment availability or uptime
- overall equipment effectiveness (OEE)
- training hours or dollars per maintenance employee
- percent rework
- materials/labor ratio
- labor-hours/completed work order
- mean time between failures (MTBF)
- percent planned work
- percent schedule attainment
- backlog levels
- PM accomplishment
- work orders generated per PM activity

*Maintenance parts inventory.* Due to the strong interrelationship between maintenance and stores, both groups should have an interest in evaluating stores performance. Potential indicators are:

- inventory value and growth
- number of inventory line items and growth
- percent or number of stockouts
- percent inactive or obsolete inventory
- MRO value as a percent of RAV
- turns per year
- inventory accuracy

### Qualitative Indicators

The quantitative indicators just listed are driven by maintenance and stores practices. Typically an individual indicator will be impacted by a group of practices, rather than a single one. Common practices that might be considered for benchmarking or process mapping include the following:

- maintenance planning and scheduling techniques and procedures
- use of computerized maintenance management systems
- work order flows or processing
- preventive maintenance procedures (for specific types of equipment)
- predictive maintenance procedures (specific technologies for specific equipment)
- training methodologies
- concurrent engineering techniques
- organizational alignments or structures
- roles and responsibilities
- improvement strategies
- participative management or self-managing team concepts
- operator performance of minor maintenance
- problem-solving methodologies
- bar coding
- parts receipt
- use of blanket agreements
- cycle counting techniques
- vendor stocking programs (VSP)
- electronic data interchange (EDI)
- use of mini or satellite stores
- parts staging and delivery methods
- tool management

Obviously the different activities discussed in the various chapters of this book are all items that organizations can benchmark with one another. As the networking relationship between plants deepens, opportunities to evaluate increasingly minute items or practices will increase. The involvement of workers in the networking activities will generate greater motivation and lead to the development of a learning organization.

# 10
# Successful TPM Companies

North American successes in TPM have been limited, but are on the rise. No plant has yet achieved the JIPM PM Prize, although several companies are considering pursuing the award. Although TPM is more than 20 years old in Japan, it has been practiced in North America for less than 10 years.

Despite its relative youth in North America, many companies are adopting its concepts fully and are implementing it vigorously in their plants and facilities. Other companies are encountering TPM while benchmarking against their Japanese competitors. Many of those organizations are experimenting with the concept in a number of locations. Japanese operations transplanted to North America also are implementing it here.

Several North American companies are now members of JIPM through direct agreements or joint ventures with Japanese and other foreign firms. This membership allows for sharing of ideas as well as access to JIPM training resources. In many cases JIPM has arranged for plant visits by North American groups to Japanese winners of the PM Prize.

Below are some North American companies that are currently involved in the TPM process.

## E. I. DuPont

DuPont, one of the premier chemical companies, has mostly continuous process plants manufacturing hydrocarbon-based chemicals, plastics, fibers, and petroleum products. It is established worldwide, with plants on almost every continent. DuPont is widely recognized for its outstanding safety record as well as its vigorous approach to benchmarking.

As a result of studying outside companies, DuPont learned of the TPM process before most other North American companies. The company organized an internal staff function, the Corporate Maintenance Leadership Team (CMLT), and gave it responsibility for helping plants improve the equipment management function. The CMLT participated in a 1987 "Best of the Best" benchmark study of maintenance practices of European and Japanese companies. The results of the benchmark concluded that the U.S.-based plants:

- had higher maintenance costs
- made less use of contractors
- had less support staff
- had much higher levels of maintenance spare parts

DuPont as a corporation decided that maintenance needed to be viewed strategically in order for it to support overall corporate goals. Years before, DuPont made a similar commitment to safety. The results dramatically helped DuPont gain notoriety as one of the world's safest companies. The DuPont Cape Fear, North Carolina, plant holds the record for the longest stretch of employee hours worked without a lost time accident.

Part of DuPont's new strategic view of maintenance included the development of a vision of success and the establishment of a process to achieve that vision. The vision and process were developed by the CMLT with input from the plants. The improvement process drew heavily from the TPM process and the team's maintenance benchmarking results. DuPont uses a measure they call uptime, which tracks all sources of loss in production, much like the OEE. The company also has established an internal award system that recognizes excellence in equipment management. The award is called the Maintenance Excellence Recognition Award.

Although DuPont has made tremendous progress and recognized corporate savings in excess of $200 million per year[10] management recognizes that the company is just beginning to understand the potential of TPM. The primary efforts to date have been focused on efficient maintenance and repair, and in the future will emphasize eliminating failures and other forms of waste.

## Magnavox

Magnavox knows firsthand the rigors of Japanese competition. Twenty years ago, it was a major player in the consumer electronics industry, making radios and televisions. Unsuccessful in defending its market share in that field, it turned to a business less subject to foreign competition, the defense industry. Unfortunately, its entry coincided with the government's slashing of the defense budget, and Magnavox has had to fight for a share of a shrinking market. Its survival depends on delivering quality parts to the government at lower prices than its competitors.

TPM is not voluntary at Magnavox as management considers it a key to future success. Small group activities have pushed decision-making authority down to the lowest levels of the organization, where teams have adopted nicknames such as the "Fuzzy Wuzzies" or the "Stack Maniacs." Each phase of the TPM process has promoted a theme. For example, the initial cleaning activity was called "Operation Clean Sweep." TPM has been embraced as one of the keys to survival.

10. V.J. Flynn, "Evolution of DuPont's Corporate Management Leadership Team." Paper presented at the 1991 TPM World Congress: Tokyo, Japan

## Texas Instruments

Texas Instruments (TI)[11] makes electrical components, microchips, and assemblies as well as specialty metals and motor controls. Its managers first learned of the TPM process in 1986. Forced to compete head to head with the Japanese in many areas, TI continually studies Japanese manufacturing techniques and philosophies.

TPM is seen by TI as a potential answer to some unique maintenance situations. In the microchip production process, many operations take place in a "clean room" controlled-atmosphere environment. Access to the clean rooms is limited, and the entry of maintenance personnel introduced additional sources of contamination to the sensitive processes. Autonomous maintenance is seen as a method of lowering the total number of entries into the clean room by allowing the production operators to perform many of the routine maintenance procedures.

TI has empowered a corporate staff with responsibility for promoting TPM in each of their plants. The responsibility of the corporate group is to prepare generic processes, disseminate information, educate and train personnel, and coordinate the total corporate TPM effort.

Significant changes took place as TI implemented TPM.

1. Modifications were made to the plant infrastructure.
2. Identified shortcomings in operator training led to the development of detailed training programs.
3. The unavailability of information for analyzing equipment performance necessitated the purchase and implementation of a computerized maintenance management system.
4. The need for better quality of spare parts led to a decision to make certain parts in-house.
5. The need to better control parts led to the establishment of a decentralized spare parts crib operation controlled by a centralized, computerized inventory control system.

---

11. James Armstrong, "TPM: A Learning Experience." TPM Conference and Exposition, 1991.

6. Customer focus by TPM teams resulted in the plant's reorganizing into production cells managed by an area manager.

Despite heavy emphasis on these activities, TI reports that it is still several years away from full implementation at the plants within the Materials and Controls group. Acceptance of the TPM process within TI operations management is mixed. TI found it necessary to report quantitative results from pilot areas in an attempt to get management "on board." Operations management also has been allowed to change the process to meet particular needs of the area or plant. This ability to customize the process has increased feelings of ownership.

Results from the TPM process at the TI pilots have been impressive. TI reports that:

- equipment productivity has improved by 50 to 80 percent
- spare part costs are reduced by 20 to 30 percent
- maintenance breakdown labor decreased by 67 percent
- lead times have been cut by 50 to 75 percent
- on-time deliveries have increased from 50 percent to 95 percent

TI reports the following lessons learned:

- Both technical (hard) and team-building (soft) training were critical to the TPM process.
- The change to a decentralized area-based organizational structure reduced bureaucracy far more than was expected.
- In analyzing and documenting maintenance tasks that were to be turned over to production operators, changes in procedures were made that greatly improved safety, quality, and productivity.
- TPM was easily accepted by the production operators and maintenance craftspeople. The most difficult persons to sell on TPM were the group leaders and supervisors.
- Managers became interested in TPM after they were exposed to quantifiable results.
- Maintenance engineering started the TPM process and played a leadership role, until implementation of the new, decentralized infrastructure. Then production management stepped in to lead the process.

Even though TPM has been successful at TI, the company does not consider the process complete. Further challenges lie ahead for both the TPM-capable plants and plants that are still in a pilot stage. Operating in an industry that changes quickly and with little notice, TI is using TPM to develop a manufacturing philosophy that works in conjunction with its research, product development, and distribution business sectors.

## Kodak

Historically, Eastman Kodak Company was a powerful company with a strong reputation for success. At one time it completely dominated the photography and imaging business, and also managed a successful side business in chemical processing. Its little yellow boxes of film were recognized as a quality product backed by a quality company

In the mid-1980s a company from Japan called Fuji began to challenge Kodak on its home turf. Fuji steadily gained market share in the 1980s and began to exercise its marketing might. While Kodak was undergoing a massive reduction in force at Kodak Park in Rochester, New York, in response to dwindling market share, Fuji pulled off a major marketing coup by sponsoring the 1984 Summer Olympics in Los Angeles. The Fuji blimp was flying over Kodak's home turf.

Kodak was startled, bewildered, and demoralized. In an attempt to turn things around, the company began to scrutinize the maintenance function. Major efforts were made to improve efficiency by implementing maintenance planning systems.

Meanwhile, a Kodak division in Tennessee (Tennessee Eastman) was learning about TPM.[12] Tennessee Eastman operates a 70-year-old chemical processing facility employing over 11,000 workers in Kingsport, Tennessee. In 1956 it licensed a manufacturing process to a Japanese firm. In the mid-1980s, the Japanese product was

---

12. W.R. Garwood, "This Warranty Expires Without Proper Maintenance." Paper presented at the 1990 International Maintenance Conference.

considered the best product on the market. Kodak visited the plant in Japan to see what design changes had been made to the process to improve the product. The team was embarrassed to learn that the Japanese had not improved the production process, but had only improved the capability and reliability of equipment through the use of superior equipment management processes.

The Kodak team returned with new ideas about equipment management, maintenance, and process capability. Soon after the visit, the plant began to actively study TPM. Significant plant resources were devoted to implementing the process. Over 600 small group activity teams were formed, empowered, and trained. Although the investment has been huge, so have the benefits. An investment in one manufacturing process of $5 million resulted in a 12 percent increase in production worth $16 million in annual profits.

It remains to be seen whether the rest of Kodak follows Tennessee Eastman in application of TPM. Challenges confronting the corporation are daunting, and have led the board of directors to make changes of personnel in the company's highest positions. Hopefully, the new management team will recognize fully that shareholder value can be increased by expanding the TPM manufacturing strategy.

## Future of TPM in North America

Numerous other companies in North America such as Ford Motor Company (as evidenced by the Charleville plant's winning the PM Prize in 1994), Procter & Gamble, and even the U.S. Postal Service are investigating and experimenting with the potential of TPM. Although pockets of success are surfacing, complete implementations and successes have yet to be attained.

Despite its modest beginnings, the authors believe that TPM will exponentially grow in importance in North America over the next decade and become the dominant strategy for equipment and reliability improvement. Where TPM has been introduced to the plant floor workers and supported by all levels of management, it has been enthusiastically embraced on the plant floor with unprecedented results. As more and more pockets of success surface, middle management will recognize TPM's power and fully support the process. Many companies and plants will soon adopt TPM as corporate or plant policy and actively deploy the process. Successes will be studied and replicated at other companies and sites. TPM will continue to grow in popularity in North America and will be continually improved by those practicing the process.

North America has a tremendous trump card to play in the global manufacturing world. Without a doubt, North America has the most enthusiastic and creative workforce in the world. TPM can and will help to harness that enthusiasm and creativity through teamwork and cooperation to achieve common goals. Those who practice TPM will continually improve the process and make the North American TPM experience the best in the world.

# *Appendix:*
# Typical TPM Master Plan

A typical master plan for implementing TPM is included on the following pages. First is a listing of the process milestones that could be included on a TPM master schedule. Following the plan milestones is a list of year-by-year goals for a typical TPM master plan. These can be used as a guide in the development of a plant-specific TPM master plan.

## Process Milestones

1. Achieve stability in the fundamentals of maintenance management, including preventive maintenance, work order systems, historical data collection, and maintenance planning.
2. Complete a plant feasibility study to establish baseline indicators of OEE, employee involvement, and equipment supplier relationships.
3. Complete TPM overview training for plant and union management.

4. Formulate a TPM implementation strategy—training methods, inspirational methods, results measurement.
5. Complete a detailed TPM implementation plan—activity schedules, budget guidelines and authority, roles and responsibilities, and outside resources.
6. Establish a specific set of measurable TPM goals in terms of OEE, employee involvement, manufacturing cycle times, inventories, customer satisfaction, and equipment supplier involvement.
7. Introduce TPM to all plant personnel and launch TPM implementation strategy—overview and OEE training.
8. Complete development of TPM training modules—single-point lessons in both process and technical skills.
9. Complete development of initial cleaning, inspection, and lubrication standards—levels one through three of autonomous maintenance.
10. Complete expanded technical skills training for operators—training to be performed by maintenance craftspeople.
11. Complete expanded failure analysis/root cause analysis—train maintenance trades people in these analytical skills and methods.
12. Establish total life cycle costing as a criteria for new equipment purchases—include collection of data from production groups and vendors to help in this decision support process.
13. Achieve complete autonomous maintenance by operators—complete levels four through seven of the autonomous maintenance process.
14. Celebrate successes achieved—have an outside resource audit the process for achievement of a predetermined level of excellence.

## Year-by-Year TPM Goals and Objectives

### Purpose

The following year-by-year goals suggest typical timing for achievement of TPM objectives in an average-size North American plant (750 to 3,000 total plant population). Smaller plants should be able to accelerate the process and larger plants may require additional time to reach the generic goals that are shown. When modifying the generic goals for a specific location, remember that the purpose of the TPM process is to provide a method to improve present plant performance with the goal of achieving zero defects, zero accidents, zero environmental compliance incidents, and zero downtime. Nothing less is acceptable performance.

## Suggested Internal Plant Communication

The following is a suggested internal plant memo to announce the start of the journey to TPM.

> In accordance with the corporate strategy of continuous improvement, plant and union management have agreed to deploy total productive maintenance (TPM) in all areas of our plant. We are committed to becoming a best-in-class operation, and we are convinced that TPM will pave the way toward achieving that goal. In support of TPM, the plant has organized a TPM deployment committee to provide management support and guidance in the TPM process. Mr. John Doe, our plant manager, will act as TPM champion. He has committed to provide, within reason, any and all resources required to ensure success of the process. Each area of the plant will have TPM coordinators who will act as facilitators, trainers, coaches, and evaluators. They will report directly to the area manager. Reporting to our TPM deployment committee will be subcommittees with specific areas of responsibility. To date the following subcommittees have been established:
> - measurables subcommittee
> - training subcommittee
> - communications subcommittee
> - small group activity organization subcommittee

Other subcommittees will be formed as the needs are identified.

We intend to implement the TPM process in all plant areas in a sequenced manner. Some areas of the plant will lead the process. Individual areas will progress through TPM at varying rates depending on the degree of customization that is required.

The plant TPM deployment committee will act as self-evaluators during the implementation process. Progress will be measured against the attached schedule of activities and the indicators developed for the process. Overall equipment effectiveness for equipment, manufacturing lines, and areas will be calculated on a regular basis and displayed for all to see on activity boards strategically placed throughout the plant.

The plant TPM deployment committee will conduct annual reviews of the process in each plant area and provide evaluations on strengths and deficiencies.

The TPM deployment committee will seek outside recognition of our progress.

## Year One Goals

First-year goals encompass the readiness of the organization to support the plant TPM process. Typically these goals can be accomplished in three to six months for an average-size plant. The reference to year one is indicative of the typical time it takes plants to achieve these goals, given that some repairs or modifications to the existing plant systems may be required before embarking on the road to TPM.

- Establishment of TPM goals and objectives for the plant with overall plans for their achievement. This includes a TPM mission statement that is developed, signed, and published by the TPM deployment committee.
- Establishment of a plant TPM deployment committee consisting of the plant TPM champion and area coordinators as well as representatives from engineering, finance, the union(s), and safety.
- Completion of a plant visit to a TPM-capable plant by selected members of the TPM deployment committee. The purpose of the trip is to learn about the power of the process and to transform the visitors into disciples of TPM.

- Establishment of full-time area TPM coordinators to facilitate and coordinate all TPM activities in the plant.
- Completion of TPM overview training given to all plant personnel by members of the TPM deployment committee. The training will impart a basic understanding of the TPM process to all plant personnel.
- Development of an overall plant TPM strategy, endorsed by the plant TPM deployment committee.

## Year Two Goals

The plant TPM deployment committee will review the status of the plant's TPM process in detail on an annual basis. An outside perspective may be required to provide an unbiased assessment. At the end of year two for an average-size plant, the plant should demonstrate satisfactory achievement of the following elements:

- Establishment of basic policies/goals/objectives/guidelines/ processes focusing on safety, equipment management, total employee involvement/empowerment, and the "concept of zero."
- Continual growth of the plant TPM organizational structure with a champion, TPM deployment committee, subcommittees, and small groups to plan, promote, train, perform, and monitor/evaluate the program's progress.
- Development of detailed plans that are endorsed by both the company and union(s) as the TPM master plan.
- Management and union commitment/support for all basic TPM concepts including small group activities, single-point lessons, autonomous maintenance, and performance measurement.
- Completion of overview and detailed TPM training for all plant employees.
- Definition of training and education needs for production, maintenance, engineering, and management personnel.
- Steps one through three of autonomous maintenance started in at least one of the plant areas.

- Suggestion or improvement idea programs initiated or expanded so that employee participation increases by a minimum of 50 percent as measured by the number of suggestions or ideas submitted.
- Achievement of an effective, basic level of equipment performance.
- Initiation of an equipment supplier involvement program to handle all new plant equipment purchases, using the concepts of total life cycle costing and the involvement of operators and maintenance personnel.
- Equipment total life cycle costing calculated for all existing and proposed equipment purchases.

## Year Three Goals

The TPM deployment committee will review the status of the plant's TPM implementation. The plant should demonstrate satisfactory achievement of the following:

- All plant personnel are aware of the TPM implementation status and how it has affected or will affect their jobs.
- Small group activities are started in all plant areas. All small groups are collecting and reporting performance measures.
- Emergency call-out maintenance is reduced to less than 1 percent of the total maintenance effort.
- A minimum of 20 percent of all maintenance effort is spent on predictive maintenance and failure mode analysis.
- The plant suggestion program triples the volume of suggestions.
- Autonomous maintenance activities (steps one through three) are started in all plant areas. Initial cleaning, preventive cleaning measures, periodic maintenance checks, and cleaning and lubrication standards exist for all plant equipment. Some plant areas will have embarked on steps four through seven of autonomous maintenance.
- Production operators perform all routine checks, lubrications, and adjustments not requiring sophisticated tools.

- All plant equipment conforms to standards developed by small groups performing autonomous maintenance for lubrication and cleanliness.
- Supplier relationships progress from new equipment purchases to older plant equipment. The original equipment suppliers are involved in equipment upgrades and add the experiences of other users of the same equipment. Equipment suppliers use examples from the plant as models for relationships with other customers.
- Machine performance indicators are expanded to include data collection to allow for analysis of repair and overhaul cycles, repair or replace decisions, and other machine-related decisions. The difference between fixing symptoms and correcting root causes is well understood by all plant personnel. Root causes are addressed to apply permanent fixes to chronic problems.
- TPM training focuses on technical skills enhancement rather than on soft process training. Training is developed and delivered by small groups with plant staff playing a support role. The major training method is use of single-point lessons.
- Activity boards are prominently displayed throughout the plant. Boards include not only performance data, but TPM process-related data tracking, training results, historical resolution of machine problems, before and after pictures, improvement themes, awards, goals, and team commitments.
- The plant decides how it will formally certify and audit its process and results.

## Year Four Goals

The plant TPM deployment committee should review the progress of the plant's TPM process and results. The plant should demonstrate satisfactory performance in the following:

- Workplace housekeeping and cleanliness are excellent. Internal and external contamination are controlled through normal daily activities rather than irregular, extraordinary cleanup efforts.

- All equipment failures are fully examined to identify and rectify root causes. Repetitive failures are virtually eliminated.
- Preventive and predictive maintenance activities undergo continuous evaluation and optimization.
- Roles of maintenance craftspeople are expanded into engineering. Craftspeople spend a minimum of 25 percent of their time examining and designing methods to increase equipment performance through modifications of equipment, process, or materials.
- All small group activity meetings are fully implemented, self-directed, and self-sustaining with no external stimulus.
- The skills of the production operators have been expanded to include basic cleaning, lubrication, adjusting, replacement of wear parts, and simple diagnostic techniques. A certification mechanism is in place to certify production operators in their new skills.
- Single-point lessons are fully operational. Technical single-point lessons are being developed, delivered, and administered by the small groups. A system is in place to share the lessons developed by one group with others.
- An integrated maintenance management system is in place and fully operational. Automated scheduling of preventive and predictive maintenance activities according to equipment needs is accomplished. Equipment history record keeping is automated to the extent that performance is easily correlated to activities and operating conditions.
- Reliability and maintainability data is stored in a database with a feedback system to equipment suppliers (OEM). Equipment suppliers are feeding information from other users of the equipment back to the plant so that equipment performance is maximized.
- Plant equipment performance indicators are expanded to encompass the whole plant, not just process equipment. Support equipment such as HVAC, boilers, utility distribution, and office equipment are included in equipment performance reports. Improvements in the performance of nonprocess equipment are documented.

- A decision on recognition of performance is investigated and determined. An external audit mechanism or award criteria is established and agreed upon. Work is begun on documenting evidence of achievements.
- Plans are established to improve areas where weaknesses have been identified by the plant TPM deployment committee.

## Year Five Goals

The plant TPM deployment committee in conjunction with an outside auditing organization will review the progress of the plant's TPM process. The plant TPM team should demonstrate satisfactory achievement of the following:

- The plant has achieved the concept of zero in accidents, breakdowns, environmental incidents, and rejects. The zero state is stable for at least six months in a number of the plant areas. Bringing the whole plant to a constant state of zero is within reach.
- All plant personnel are participating in some form of small group activities or self directed work teams. The members exhibit enthusiasm and understanding of the process.
- Production operators have assumed all minor and repetitive maintenance task responsibilities. Maintenance skilled crafts-people have assumed the majority of the maintenance engineering functions and have assumed responsibility for constantly improving the equipment.
- Work organization, material organization, facility cleanliness, and workplace morale show marked improvement. Before and after pictures, attitude surveys, and other measures document improvements.
- Equipment life cycle cost is lowered and the improvement is documented through plant records.
- All TPM deficiencies are documented, with corrective action plans developed to address each of them.
- Documented evidence clearly shows the plant is at world class performance levels.

- The plant is recognized by an independent auditing group as being TPM-capable.
- The plant is regularly visited by other plants and companies as an example of a TPM-capable plant. The plant willingly shares the process in return for opinions, comments, and benchmarking information from the visiting organizations.

# About the Authors

Charles Robinson has developed a national reputation as an expert in total productive maintenance and in developing corporate strategies in equipment reliability. He trained in Japan under Seiichi Nakajima and Kunio Shirose of the Japan Institute of Plant Maintenance. As a consultant since 1976, he has helped implement TPM at major corporations including Ford Motor Company, Boeing, Ocean Spray, Exxon, Fluor Daniel, TRW, Rockwell, Lawrence Livermore, Nissan, Isuzu, Toyota, Shell, Texaco, Mobil, British Petroleum, USAF, Conoco, and others. He has authored articles for *Plant Services, Maintenance Technology, Plant Engineering, AIPE Journal,* and *IMI Newsletter,* and has been a featured speaker at industry conferences, both national and regional.

Andrew Ginder has earned a national reputation as a consultant specializing in maintenance and equipment reliability. Since 1979, he has assisted Ford Motor Company in developing its process for maintenance excellence (PME) and has supported many companies worldwide to optimize their maintenance practices and equipment reliability, including Elkem Metals, Weyerhaeuser, BASF, Hercules, Exxon, Hoechst-Celanese, Texaco, Hewlett-Packard, Arco Chemical, Allied Signal, Lever Brothers, and Pennzoil Products. Mr. Ginder has published numerous articles in industry journals such as *Maintenance Technology, Hydrocarbon Processing,* and *Engineer's Digest,* and has often spoken at national and regional maintenance conferences.

# Index

A.T. Kearney, Inc., 13
American Institute of Plant Engineers (AIPE), 13
American Institute for Total Productive Maintenance (AITPM), 13, 24
American manufacturing, history of, 11
Autonomous inspection, 109–12
  guidelines for, 109–10
Autonomous maintenance, 57–62, 94–116
  initial barriers to, 59
  seven levels of, 57, 94
    autonomous inspection, 109–12
    development of cleaning and lubrication standards, 104

Autonomous maintenance (cont.)
  general inspection, 107–109
  independent autonomous maintenance, 116–17
  initial cleaning, 94–99
  preventive cleaning measures, 99–104
  process discipline, 112–16
  work activity changes resulting from, 61
Availability, 125–28
  defined, 126

Benchmarking, 161
  choosing a team for, 164–65
  cross-industry networking groups and, 166–69
  defined, 162
  finding a partner for, 163–64

Benchmarking (cont.)
  in-depth observation and,
    165–66
  one-time visits and, 163
  qualitative, 169–70
  quantitative, 169
Better-than-new environment, 106
Bodek, Norman, ix

Camp, Robert, 161
Cleaning and lubrication standards,
    development of, 104
  steps for, 105–106
Closed-loop measurement, 4
Commissioning, 83
Company strategy progression, 37
Compensation, 120
Computerized maintenance man-
    agement system (CMMS),
    69–71, 73–75, 109
Constraints. *See* Theory of con-
    straints
Continuous flow manufacturing
    (CFM), 2
  defined, 152
  goal of, 152–54
  terms used in, 153
Cost reporting system, 30–31
Cross-industry networking,
    166–69
Culture of organization, 6–7

Disposal, 83
E.I. DuPont, 174–75

Early equipment management
    program, 83–87
  phases of, 83–87
Eastman Kodak Company,
    178–79
Employee empowerment, 3–4
Employee involvement, 3
Equipment effectiveness, 47–57
Equipment history system, 30

Equipment loss, 125
  elements for tracking, 125
  types of, 125
Equipment management life cycle
    chart, 88
Equipment selection, 49

Ford Motor Company, 17
  PM Excellence Award, 16, 75
  Q1 quality process, 45–46
Frustration during TPM develop-
    ment, 39
Fuji Film, 17, 178
Fundamental maintenance prac-
    tices, 28–31
  cost reporting system, 30–31
  equipment history system, 30
  work authorization system, 29
  work identification system, 29
  work order system, 29–30

General inspection, 107–109
  developing standards for,
    107–108
*The Goal*, 152
Goldratt, Eliyahu, 152

HSB Reliability Technologies, 13

Ideal cycle time, 129–32
In-depth observation, benefits of,
    165–66
Independent autonomous main-
    tenance, 116–17
Initial cleaning, 94–99
  guidelines for performing,
    95–97
Initial TPM assessment, 28
Institute of Industrial Engineers
    (IIE), 13
International Maintenance Insti-
    tute (IMI), 13
Investment, 153
  decreasing, 153

Japan Institute of Plant Mainte-
nance (JIPM), 1
background of, 12
TPM process, 21-22
Japan Management Association
Group (JMA), 12
structure, 13
Japanese perception of American
work habits, 11
Jardine, Dr. Andrew, 63
JIPM award, 14

Kodak. *See* Eastman Kodak
Company
Kvaerner Engineering, 63

Labor union endorsement of
TPM, 123
Labor unions and TPM, 119–24
Living document, 40

Magnavox, 175
Maintenance prevention (MP),
65–66
*Maintenance Technology* maga-
zine, 13
Malcolm Baldrige National
Quality Award, 14

Nakajima, Seiichi, 1, 12
Negative sentiment, dealing with,
35–36
Net available time, 126
Net operating rate, 133–34
Net profit, 153
Nippondenso, 1, 12
Not-invented-here (NIH) syn-
drome, 11, 161

OEE. *See* Overall equipment effectiveness
One-point lessons. *See* Single-
point lessons
On-the-job training, 110

Operating expense, 153
decreasing, 153
Operating time, 126, 133
Operation, 83
Optimus software, 63
Organizational culture, 6–7
Overall equipment effectiveness
(OEE), 8, 19
and autonomous maintenance,
98
calculation for line or process,
137–38
calculation for single machine,
135–36
correlated to financial results,
48
power of, 149
steps to improve, 49–53
showing results of, 148–49
as TPM indicator, 47–57
types of equipment loss, 125
Overall machine effectiveness
(OME). *See* Overall
equipment effectiveness
Overseer group, 25

Performance efficiency, 125,
128–34
Performance-based assessment, 7
Periodicals of interest, 13
Planned downtime, 126
Planned maintenance system
transition table, 67
Planned maintenance system,
62–75
*Plant Engineering* magazine, 13
Plant OEE calculation, 144–48
PM Prize. *See* TPM Excellence
Award
Predictive maintenance (PdM),
62, 64–65
Preventive cleaning measures,
99–104
external factors and, 103–104

Preventive cleaning measures (cont.)
    process excess and, 101–103
    process leaks and, 100–101
Preventive maintenance (PM), 64
Process discipline, 112–16
    objectives for, 112
    procedures to examine for, 113
Process leaks, 100–101
Procurement, 83
Productivity, 153

Qualitative benchmarking, 169–70
    indicators for, 171–72
Quality losses, accounting for,
        138–44
Quality rate, 125, 134–35
Quantitative benchmarking, 169
    indicators for, 170–71

Reactive maintenance (RM), 64
Return on investment, 153

Single-point lessons, 77. See also
        Skills training
Skills training, 75–83
    coaching and, 80
    communications workshops
        and, 76, 77–80
    group dynamics and, 76
    maintenance systems and, 77
    single-point lessons, 77–78
    skill certification and, 81–83
    video aids for, 80–81
Small groups, 53–57
    defined, 54–55
    formation of, 55–56
    guidelines for decision making
        in, 56–57
Society of Maintenance and Reli-
        ability Professionals
        (SMRP), 13, 24
Specification, 83
Speed ratio, 133
Startup, 83
Strategic focus, 7

Texas Instruments, 176–77
Theory of constraints (TOC),
        154–56
    correlation with TPM, 159–60
    and process industry, 156–59
Throughput, 153
    increasing, 154
Total available time, 126
Total defects, 134
Total parts run, 132–33, 134
Total productive maintenance
        (TPM)
    decision to implement, 5–7
    defined, 2
    maintenance in, 4–5
Toyota Motor Company, 1, 12
TPM and TQM, 18
TPM celebration, 43–44, 88–91
TPM committee organization
        chart, 32
TPM committee structure, 31–32
TPM deployment committee,
        25–26, 28
    characteristics of members, 26
    frustration in, 39
    initial responsibility of, 28
    plan development method and,
        40–41
    size of, 26
    structure chart of, 27,
TPM deployment plan, 31
TPM development, frustration
        during, 39
TPM Excellence Award, 14
    criteria for score, 15
    recipients of, 16
TPM implementation time peri-
        od, 45
TPM kickoff activities, 41–44
TPM master plan, 38
    example of, 181–90
TPM process
    companies involved in,
        174–79
    JIPM's steps, 21-22

TPM process (cont.)
steps in implementing, 46–91
step 7, improve equipment effectiveness, 47–57
step 8, implement autonomous maintenance, 57–62
step 9, planned maintenance system, 62–75
step 10, training to improve skills, 75–83
step 11, early equipment management program, 83–87
step 12, perfect TPM implementation and raise TPM levels, 87–91
steps in preparing for, 21–44
step 1, educational campaign, 23–25
step 2, organizational structure, 25–32
step 3, announcement, 32–36

TPM process (cont.)
step 4, establish basic policies and goals, 36–38
step 5, master plan for implementation, 38–41
step 6, kick off TPM, 41–44
TPM World Congress, 16–20
TQM, TPM and, 18
Training. *See* Skills training

Unions. *See* Labor unions
Unplanned downtime, 127
U.S. Postal Service, 17

Variable expense, 153

Work authorization system, 29
Work identification system, 29
Work order system, 29–30
Work-flow diagram, 115
Worker benefits, 120

CPSIA information can be obtained at www.ICGtesting.com
Printed in the USA
LVOW060114040112

262235LV00001B/104/A